# Outdoors in Arizona
## A Guide to Camping

**ARIZONA**
**HIGHWAYS BOOK**

James Tallon

*Text by*
**Bob Hirsch**

*Around the Campfire Stories by*
**Marshall Trimble**

*Illustrations by*
**Joe Beeler**

*Photographs by*
**Arizona Highways Contributors**

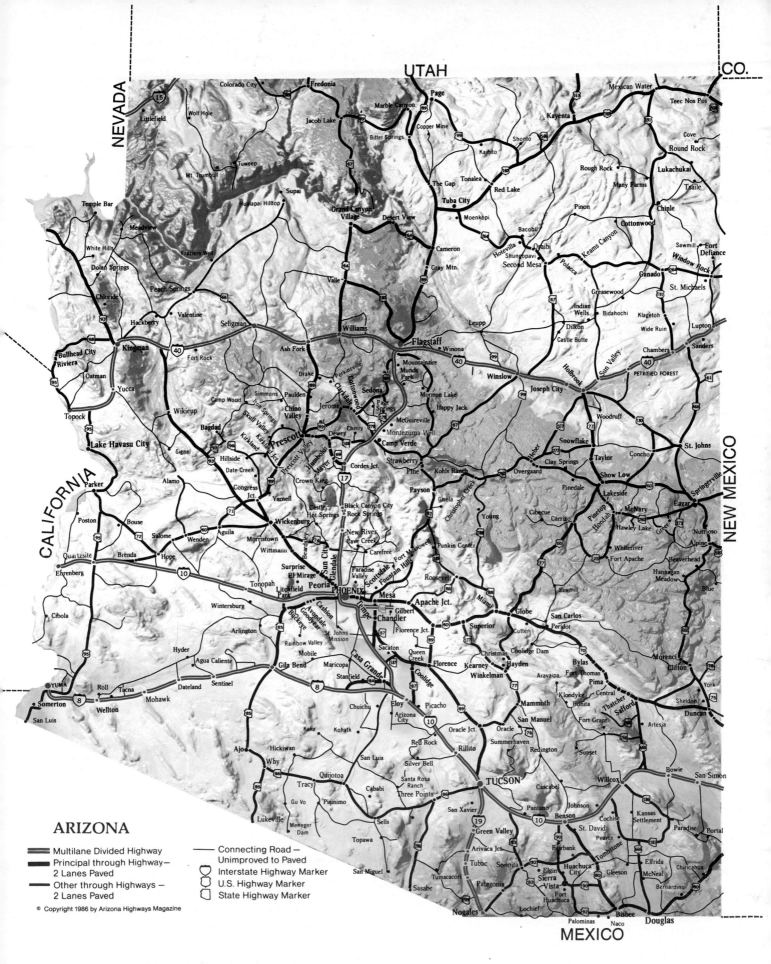

## ARIZONA

Multilane Divided Highway
Principal through Highway—
2 Lanes Paved
Other through Highways —
2 Lanes Paved

Connecting Road —
Unimproved to Paved
Interstate Highway Marker
U.S. Highway Marker
State Highway Marker

© Copyright 1986 by Arizona Highways Magazine

*Family campsite near Flagstaff. Jerry Sieve*

3

# Regions

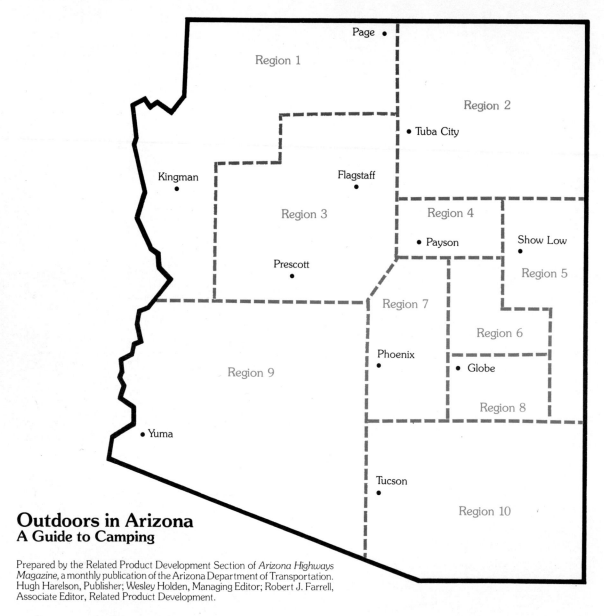

Region 1

Page •

Region 2

• Tuba City

Kingman •

Flagstaff •

Region 3

Region 4

Payson •

Show Low •

Region 5

Prescott •

Region 7

Region 6

Phoenix •

• Globe

Region 9

Region 8

• Yuma

Tucson •

Region 10

## Outdoors in Arizona
### A Guide to Camping

Prepared by the Related Product Development Section of *Arizona Highways Magazine,* a monthly publication of the Arizona Department of Transportation. Hugh Harelson, Publisher; Wesley Holden, Managing Editor; Robert J. Farrell, Associate Editor, Related Product Development.

*Staff for this book:*

**J. PETER MORTIMER — Editor**
**JAMES R. METCALF — Design and Production**
**MERRILL WINDSOR — Associate Editor**

Library of Congress Catalog Number 85-072739
ISBN 0-916179-06-0

Printed in Japan

*For readers' convenience,* Outdoors in Arizona: A Guide to Camping *is organized by geographical regions as indicated above. For this contents map, regional boundaries have been approximated and irregularities squared off. A more precise regional map appears within each chapter. Campsite tent symbols ⬢ are placed on the maps as near as possible to the actual location.*

# Contents

# Camping Arizona Style

Let's suppose you are spending a spring night in the Arizona desert, tucked in a sleeping bag and rolled in a tarp, blinking at stars that blaze with a brilliance never seen in the city. The rock that digs into your hip (you thought you'd picked the ground clean!) was formed a million years ago. The saguaro silhouetted against the night sky has seen 200 springs come and go. It has seen, too, the humans who have been here before you: Indians and explorers, padres and prospectors, cowboys, and the noisy mechanized visitors of recent times.

The breeze has carried away countless songs, conversations, and boasts, and it will still blow softly when you are gone. After a while the rain will come and collect in the hollow made by your sleeping body, and wildflowers will grow where the extra moisture collects. The rain will carry away ashes of your campfire, and there will remain no trace of your passing.

So, in the language of bureaucracy, camping is "nonconsumptive." That unattractive word stands for a very attractive concept — and an unequal relationship: You "consume" nothing and are rewarded with everything. True succor for your mind and body; healing sights and sounds and sensations, stored in your memory where they can be recalled a thousand times.

Sometimes everything works just right and a pleasant recollection on Thursday triggers plans for an outing the following Saturday. Wise campers stock up, too, with moments of deep peace that they can use to ease daily frustrations. If you're late for work and freeway traffic grinds to a halt, you can close your eyes and spend a few seconds on Lake Powell, anchored in some lonesome canyon 30 miles from the nearest road. No noisy machines, just soaring rock of strawberry hue, arching blue sky, and darker blue water whispering against the hull. Or let your mind rest on a bed of springy pine needles among the ponderosas, south of Flagstaff, savoring the smell of wood smoke and frying bacon. No stress on earth can completely resist such powerful spells.

Arizona campers are a widely divergent group. Backpackers look down their noses at tenters who don't pull up stakes every day. Tent campers think the folks who favor travel trailers are simply parking a home on wheels, while the trailer clan believe those who drive motor homes are too hedonistic to qualify as real campers.

But in truth, all of them have a great deal in common — especially their delight in the Arizona outdoors. There are obvious differences between a backpacker teasing a tiny flame into life so he can heat water for morning coffee and the motor home occupant punching a button to start the generator so the microwave oven can do its job in 90 seconds. But who is to say which of these campers will get the most from the outing — who will jump back into the upstream rapids of daily life most refreshed and renewed? Each person determines what is most important to him or her — there is no "average camper."

And there is no closed season. In Arizona, campers can do their thing whenever they like. Someplace in the state, every day of the year, there is a camping opportunity, a place to pitch a tent or park a recreational vehicle, a place to relax in ideal surroundings. In winter, desert campsites and the big reservoirs along the Colorado are drenched in sunshine. In summer, the tall, green pines of the high country offer a cool haven. Between those extremes are such delightful kingdoms as the Verde Valley, the Chiricahua Mountains, and the evergreen oak stands of Peña Blanca and Patagonia. There is no off-season.

So the love affair between Arizona campers and the Arizona outdoors continues. We open our hearts and are shaped by the tiny events of each outing. Remember...?

—the way you hold the first cup of coffee in the early morning chill, so it warms you both inside and out;

—the velvet silence when you awaken at night in the deep woods;

—the pure-gold arrow of sunlight that has found a small tear in the tent fabric;

—a daily world record for the "dress and dash" distance between your sleeping bag and the morning campfire;

—a lazy hour's walk along the water, hand in hand;

—the certain knowledge, as you stare into the dying embers of the evening campfire, that no one, anywhere, at that certain moment, is more at peace.

*Every Arizona camping trip begins with a mixture of excitement and peacefulness; you leave ragged and unraveled and return renewed and refreshed. And it doesn't really make any difference whether you're shaded by a saguaro or a sycamore.* James Tallon

# Colorado River Country

The mighty Colorado dominates this region, and with few exceptions, the camping is water-oriented. The river winds for more than 300 miles through lonesome canyons in the northern part of the state, then becomes the Arizona-Nevada and Arizona-California border, angling southward toward the Gulf of California. Away from the water there are few towns and few people; but the big river is a watery magnet, and wherever there is access, you'll see license plates and boat stickers from all over the West and from other parts of North America as well. And if you walk through Mather campground on the South Rim of the Grand Canyon on a summer evening, you'll hear voices speaking a dozen foreign languages, all exclaiming over the wonder of the great chasm.

Although most of the campgrounds are keyed to water, the range of choices offers great variety. It's a long way in both distance and atmosphere, for example, from Jacob Lake to Alamo Lake. Jacob Lake, named for the famed Mormon explorer and trail blazer Jacob Hamblin, is a small pool hidden in the tall forests of the Kaibab Plateau at an elevation of 7900 feet. Motorists from the south cross the Colorado at Marble Canyon, then drive through the dry vastness of House Rock Valley before they make the abrupt climb from sagebrush to fir, spruce, and aspen groves. The campground is a summer place, a cool stopover for travelers to or from the North Rim of the Grand Canyon.

Alamo's elevation, on the other hand, is just 1250 feet, so the Arizona State Parks system campground on the south shore of the lake is open all year. Alamo is out in the desert west of Wickenburg and north of Wenden, and the last thirty miles to the lake will take you through open, sparse landscape. You must spend some time—sort of an apprenticeship—in this kind of country before its beauty wins you over. Then you look forward to a few days on the lakeshore, surrounded by the dark hills and sharp-sided mountains, the lake a patch of blue in the midst of shades of tan and green.

For even greater contrast, choose a boat access campground on Lake Havasu. Here, for a couple of dollars a day, you own a slice of sandy beach to park your boat and a table-bench-grill for cooking and eating. The blue-green water of Lake Havasu is your front yard and the only road to the campsite. You can fish, water ski, cruise on the big reservoir, or simply soak up the sunshine. And you can appreciate the camping diversity in this region when you realize the difference in elevation between Havasu and the Grand Canyon's North Rim is one-and-a-half miles—straight up!

That also suggests that somewhere along the Colorado, during every season of the year, there's a campground where the weather and surroundings are delightful. Wherever you choose to park your recreational vehicle or pitch your tent, there's never any doubt you are in the West. The hundred-mile views might include Wahweap Bay on Lake Powell, with red and buff battlements marking a jagged line between blue sky and blue water; the shimmering outlines of ridges and temples in the Grand Canyon, disappearing in the distance from the Desert View campground at the eastern edge of the national park; or the long, white exclamation point that is the wake of a Lake Mohave speedboat towing a mini-dot of a skier.

It is the land of the big canyon, the big river, the big lake, and the big view. Camp here once and be captured forever.

*(Above left) The campground at Lees Ferry matches the grandeur of the Colorado River and the Vermilion Cliffs.* James Tallon
*(Right) Arizona's Grand Canyon is the world's most spectacular campground; raft trips stop in a new spot each night, each more beautiful than the one before.* J. Peter Mortimer

(Above) Tent camping on the uncrowded shores of Lake Powell. Tom Bean
(Right) The campground at Lake Powell's Wahweap Bay has a million-dollar view of the bay and Castle Rock. Gary Ladd
(Below) Boat campers can choose from a thousand beaches on Lake Powell. James Tallon

(Above) Both rims of the Grand Canyon offer unique camping opportunities, especially in the uncrowded off-season. Tom Algire
(Left) Youngsters meet a friend from the wild. Inge Martin
(Right) Chow time at a North Rim camp. James Tallon
(Far right) Exploring a side road—finding a view of your own—somewhere along the North Rim. James Tallon

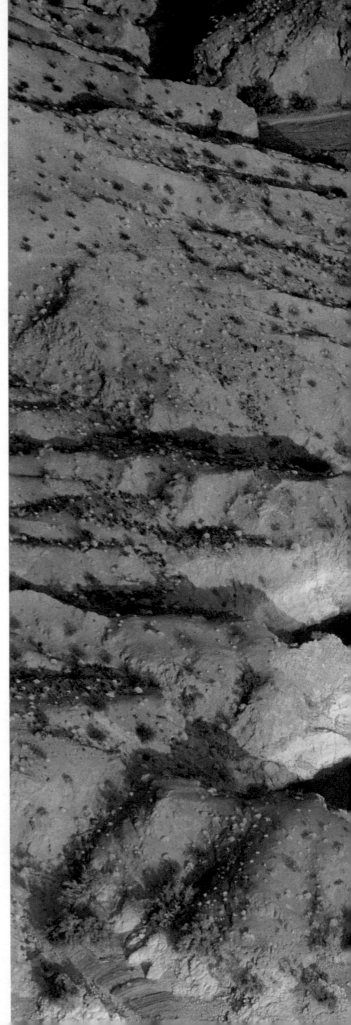

(Above) A family's "private" beach resort on Lake Mohave. James Tallon
(Right) Rental houseboats are available on all the major Colorado River lakes, and you can choose a lonesome canyon to "own" for a few days. J. Peter Mortimer
(Below) Sunshine and peace are the main attractions. J. Peter Mortimer

# Captain John Hance
## The Greatest Yarnspinner of 'em All

*Around the Campfire*

In the old days they used to say that anyone who visited the Grand Canyon and didn't meet Captain John Hance had missed half the show. For some twenty years, Cap Hance provided lying and lodging for the tourists. His brand of humor was of a windy nature. The dudes never knew just how much of Cap's stories to believe, for he always led them down the paths of plausibility until they found they'd reached conclusions that were impossible—or were they?

Like the time Cap was riding his favorite white horse, Darby, near Red Butte along the Canyon's rim. (He gave all his mounts the same name—claimed it made it easier to remember what to call them.) Now old Darby could smell hostile Indians forty miles away, and when he started tossing and snorting, Cap grew wary.

Pretty soon he saw a bunch of warriors riding hard from the south. Cap put the spurs to Darby and they turned east only to find another painted-up war party coming from that direction.

Darby set up and turned the other way, but another band was whooping it up in the west. Cap Hance and Darby knew that their only way out was to jump the Canyon. They didn't have a minute to waste. Old Darby took a running start and gave a mighty leap. Up and over the Canyon they soared. About half way across, Cap let his eyes drift downward. Several thousand feet below, the mighty Colorado looked like a tiny reddish-brown ribbon twisting and winding between the steep Canyon walls.

Old Darby got curious, too, and looked down. That brief glance caused him to lose his concentration, and they began to fall. Down they went like an elevator gone berserk. The Canyon walls were sliding by in a blur as Cap and Darby gathered speed on the descent.

Cap knew that the only way the pair could survive the fall was to pull up on old Darby. He'd trained that horse since he was a colt, and everyone agreed Darby was the best reined horse in Arizona, or the whole West for that matter.

Cap took a firm grip on those leather reins and hollered "Whoa, Darby."

Well, old Darby responded to his master's command and pulled up short just three feet from the Canyon floor.

Hance and Darby glided safely that last three feet.

Captain Hance (noboby knows why they called him captain—it just seemed to fit) first came to the Grand Canyon in the 1880s to go prospecting. Whatever luck he had as an argonaut was far outshadowed by his success as a storyteller and trail guide for the tourists who visited the Grand Canyon in those days before the arrival of the railroad.

"Why, Captain Hance, how did you lose the tip of your finger?" a tourist asked him as he was giving one of his patented lectures.

Cap paused and stared at the missing part of his finger as if noticing it for the first time, then replied, "Why, ma'am, I reckon I plumb wore off the end of that thing pointing out the purty scenery out here over the past thirty years."

The audience loved it, and from that day forth Cap Hance's reputation as a windjammer grew. Visitors who didn't get a chance to be victimized by his windies felt shortchanged. Next to the Canyon itself, Cap was the main attraction.

Sometimes Cap Hance's whoppers almost got him in a heap of trouble. Like the time a stranger asked him how the deer hunting was around the South Rim.

"Why, shucks," Cap replied, "I went out this morning and killed three all by myself."

"That's wonderful," the stranger exclaimed. "Do you know who I am?"

"No, I don't," Hance admitted.

"Well, I'm the game warden."

Undaunted, the captain snorted, "And do you know who I am?"

"No, I don't," the game warden said.

"Well," came the reply, "I'm John Hance, the biggest damn liar in these parts."

During inclement weather, a layer of dense fog sometimes fills the Canyon from rim to rim. Cap used to tell of the times when he and Darby rode across the fog bank to the North Rim. On one occasion, when they were about midway, the fog began to lift. Old Darby hurriedly jumped from one patch to another trying to reach the rim, but soon ran out of fog, slipped through a hole, and landed on top of Zoroaster Temple. Cap and Darby were marooned out on that rocky monolith for four weeks before another blanket of fog covered the Canyon.

"It was a light fog," he later recalled, "but by then old Darby and me were a whole lot lighter too."

Perhaps Cap Hance's greatest saga concerned a band of hardbitten rustlers who stole his team of prize mules. The matched set of long-eared critters was Cap's pride. There wasn't anything the mules wouldn't do for him. Naturally he was heartsick when he went out to the corral one morning and found them missing. He saddled up old Darby and rode out to pick up the trail. The outlaws had set a path towards Ash Fork, down on the Santa Fe main line about sixty miles south of the Canyon.

About sundown of the third day, Cap's keen senses picked up the smell of meat cooking over hot coals. He got off Darby and crawled over a rise for a look-see. Nestled in a thick juniper grove was an old barn. The outlaws, unaware they were being followed, had stopped to eat.

Cap's joy at catching up with the rustlers quickly turned to sorrow when he saw the hides of his prize mules nailed to the wall of the barn. Why, that pack of rascals had skinned his pets and were sitting around the fire getting ready to eat them.

There were five of the outlaws, all well armed—meanest looking scalawags you ever saw. Cap not only felt it was his duty to capture that wild bunch but also figured he owed it to his poor mules to avenge their demise!

This called for some mighty fast thinking, and Cap rose to the occasion. He waited patiently for the rustlers to fill their mouths with mule meat; then, just as they were swallowing, he hollered, "Whoa, mule!"

And would you believe it? Those obedient mules heard their master's call and stopped right in their tracks.

While those outlaws were squirming on the ground trying to clear their clogged throats, Cap Hance walked into camp and disarmed the whole bunch.

16

# Campfire Recipes

### FISH IN FOIL

Trout (or any other kind of fish) tastes best immediately after it is caught. A fish eaten an hour after it hits the net is infinitely better than one that has been in the ice chest for a day, or one that has been frozen for a month.

So plan on fish meals in camp. Cooking trout in foil is easy and the result delicious; the same technique works for bass fillets or any other fish.

Lightly salt and pepper two pan-size trout (or equivalent fillets) inside and out; add a dollop of butter to the body cavity of each. Double-wrap in foil. You could put the package right in the coals, but hot spots make exact cooking time hard to figure, so it's better to use a grill over the coals. Allow about fifteen minutes to cook the fish, turning when half that time is up.

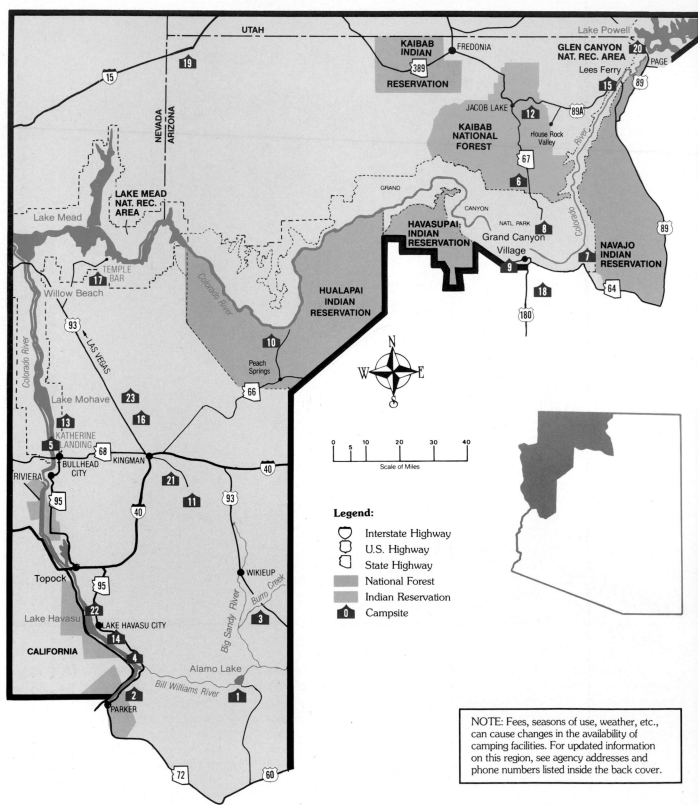

UTAH

KAIBAB INDIAN RESERVATION

FREDONIA

GLEN CANYON NAT. REC. AREA

Lake Powell

PAGE

Lees Ferry

JACOB LAKE

KAIBAB NATIONAL FOREST

House Rock Valley

NEVADA
ARIZONA

GRAND

CANYON

NATL. PARK

Colorado River

LAKE MEAD NAT. REC. AREA

Lake Mead

HAVASUPAI INDIAN RESERVATION

Grand Canyon Village

NAVAJO INDIAN RESERVATION

TEMPLE BAR

Willow Beach

Colorado River

HUALAPAI INDIAN RESERVATION

LAS VEGAS

Peach Springs

Lake Mohave

KATHERINE LANDING

BULLHEAD CITY

KINGMAN

RIVIERA

Topock

WIKIEUP

Burro Creek

Lake Havasu

LAKE HAVASU CITY

CALIFORNIA

Alamo Lake

Big Sandy River

Bill Williams River

PARKER

N W E S

0 5 10 20 30 40
Scale of Miles

Legend:

Interstate Highway
U.S. Highway
State Highway
National Forest
Indian Reservation
Campsite

NOTE: Fees, seasons of use, weather, etc., can cause changes in the availability of camping facilities. For updated information on this region, see agency addresses and phone numbers listed inside the back cover.

# Colorado River Country Campsites

The Arizona-Nevada-California portion of the Colorado River and its chain of great reservoirs is more than 500 miles long. Summer is the busy time here, with spring and fall a bit less crowded, and winter downright lonesome at many of the campgrounds. There are a few pine-forest destinations, but most campsites are in desert surroundings with rugged buttes or cliffs in view or a horizon shaped by the notches and peaks of distant ranges.

**Lake Powell**, principal feature of Glen Canyon National Recreation Area, offers boat camping all around and improved campsites at Hite, Bullfrog, and Halls Crossing marinas uplake from the big marina at **Wahweap**, a few miles north of Glen Canyon Dam and the town of Page. The National Park Service campground at Wahweap has 208 spaces, plus a late-arrival area that can handle an additional 100 vehicles. No hookups here, but water and modern restrooms plus a dump station for recreational vehicle holding tanks. Most of the sites are pull-through and furnished with table-bench units and standup grills. Picnic area and swimming beach nearby. The main marina offers free launching on a concrete ramp. Elevation is 3800 feet. Daily fee; 14-day stay limit; open all year.

**Lees Ferry** campground is administered by the National Park Service. It's laid out on a bluff overlooking the Colorado River and the site of the ferry service that was the only way to cross the Colorado in this region until Navajo Bridge was built nearby. There are 65 sites here with water, modern restrooms, table-bench-grill units, windscreens, ramadas. Fee; stay limit, 14 days. Access by paved road, 6 miles north of Marble Canyon and U.S. Route 89. The campground is open all year. Float trips through the Grand Canyon begin here.

**Jacob Lake** is in the Kaibab National Forest north of the Grand Canyon at the junction of State Route 67 (the road to the North Rim) and U.S. Route 89. Elevation is 7900 feet. The campground has 48 sites, with table-bench units, water, and modern restrooms. Fee; 14-day stay limit. Campground open from May to October. (Water is turned off early and late in the season when the danger of freezing exists.) Gas station, store, and cafe across the highway.

**Demotte** campground is on State Route 67, about 25 miles south of Jacob Lake. It offers 20 sites with water, outhouses, and table-bench units. Fee; 14-day stay limit; late May-early September season. This campground is best for tents, smaller recreational vehicles, and trailers. Elevation is 8000 feet. Beautiful autumn color in this area in early October.

**Grand Canyon: North Rim** campground is close enough to the big gorge so that a minute's walk gives you an impressive view. There are 82 scattered sites; table-bench units, water, restrooms. Elevation is 8200 feet. You are 45 miles south of Jacob Lake on State Route 67. Fee; 7-day stay limit; May-October season.

| RECREATION SITE NAME | APPROX. ELEV. | SEASONS OF USE | DAYS-LIMITS | FEE | NO. OF UNITS | SAFE WATER | 16 FT. RV LIMIT | WASTE DISP. | BOATING | FISHING |
|---|---|---|---|---|---|---|---|---|---|---|
| 1 ALAMO LAKE | 1250 | All Yr. | 14 | X | 400 | X | | X | X | X |
| 2 BUCKSKIN MTN. STATE PARK | 420 | All Yr. | 14 | X | 105 | X | | X | X | X |
| 3 BURRO CREEK | 1950 | All Yr. | 14 | X | 60 | X | | X | | |
| 4 CATTAIL COVE | 450 | All Yr. | 14 | X | 40 | X | | X | X | X |
| 5 DAVIS CAMP | 500 | All Yr. | 14-30 | X | 94 | X | | X | X | X |
| 6 DEMOTTE | 8000 | May Sep. | 14 | X | 20 | X | | | | |
| 7 DESERT VIEW | 7400 | May Oct. | 7 | X | 50 | X | | | | |
| 8 GRAND CANYON N. Rim | 8200 | May Oct. | 7 | X | 82 | X | | X | | |
| 9 GRAND CANYON (Mather) S. Rim* | 6900 | Mar. Dec. | 7 | X | 327 | X | | X | | |
| 10 HUALAPAI INDIAN RES. | 4790 | All Yr. | | X | | | | | | |
| 11 HUALAPAI MTN. PARK | 6200 | All Yr. | 14 | X | 74 | X | | | | |
| 12 JACOB LAKE* | 7900 | May Oct. | 14 | X | 48 | X | | | | |
| 13 KATHERINE LANDING | 650 | All Yr. | 30 | X | 173 | X | | X | X | X |
| 14 LAKE HAVASU BOAT ACCESS | 450 | All Yr. | 14 | X | 170 | | | | X | X |
| 15 LEES FERRY | 3200 | All Yr. | 14 | X | 65 | X | | X | X | X |
| 16 PACK SADDLE | 6200 | May Oct. | 14 | | 8 | | | | | |
| 17 TEMPLE BAR | 1280 | All Yr. | 90 | X | 153 | X | | X | X | X |
| 18 TEN-X | 6600 | May Oct. | 14 | X | 70 | X | | | | |
| 19 VIRGIN RIVER | 1900 | All Yr. | 14 | X | 124 | X | | X | | |
| 20 WAHWEAP | 3800 | All Yr. | 14 | X | 208 | X | | X | X | X |
| 21 WILD COW | 6250 | May Oct. | 14 | | 12 | | | | | |
| 22 WINDSOR BEACH | 450 | All Yr. | 14 | X | 132 | X | | | X | X |
| 23 WINDY POINT | 6100 | May Oct. | 14 | | 10 | | | | | |

*Sites with handicapped facilities.

19

# Campsites

A store, self-service laundry, showers, and gas station are nearby. Lodge and other facilities are at the rim, about 1.5 miles away. Spectacular camping!

**Grand Canyon: Mather (South Rim)** campground, administered by the National Park Service, is one of the few Arizona campgrounds where you must make a reservation (during the busy season May 15-September 30). Elevation is 6900 feet. Campground has water, modern restrooms, table-bench-grill units; 327 sites. Fee; 7-day stay limit. Mather is open March-December. Six sites for handicapped. All services at Grand Canyon Village. With the Canyon so near, this is one campground where you won't idle away your time.

**Desert View** campground is part of the national park facilities and is located on the Grand Canyon's South Rim just inside the eastern entrance to the park on State Route 64. There are 50 sites here, set in juniper and oak. Water, restrooms, fee; 7-day stay

limit. Park Service holds evening educational programs in new amphitheater. Campground is open from May to October. Desert View is used mostly by visitors coming or going, so stays are generally short.

**Ten-X** campground is in Kaibab National Forest on State Route 64-U.S. Route 180 about 49 miles north of Williams—just outside the southern entrance to Grand Canyon National Park. Campground has 70 sites set in a grove of tall ponderosa pines. Water, outhouses, table-bench units; May-October season. Fee; stay limit 14 days. Adjacent group site, **Charley Tank**, can be reserved for up to 100 campers. Fee; fire rings; table-bench units; outhouses.

**Hualapai Indian Reservation** offers some primitive camping along the south bank of the Colorado, north of State Route 66 between Seligman and Kingman. Daily camping permits are sold at the Hualapai Wildlife Department office on State Route 66.

**Virgin River** is 20 miles southwest of St. George, Utah, off Interstate 15 just inside Arizona's northern border. This Bureau of Land Management site has 124 units, safe water, and a dump station. White-water rafting and hiking in the Paiute Wilderness Area draw campers to the rocky country. Fee; 14-day stay limit; open all year. Elevation: 1900 feet.

**Temple Bar** campground is one of the Park Service facilities of Lake Mead National Recreation Area. Access is off U.S. Route 93 north of Kingman on an all-paved county road. The campground has 153 sites, water, modern restrooms, and both pull-through and back-in spaces with table-bench units and shade trees. Elevation is only 1280 feet, so summer temperatures often exceed 100 degrees. Fee; 90-day stay limit; open all year. Facilities also include a trailer park, store, cafe, marina, and launch ramp.

**Pack Saddle** and **Windy Point** campgrounds are 15 miles north of Kingman on U.S. Route 93 then a bumpy 6 miles northeast on unpaved Chloride-Big Wash Road. Pack Saddle has 8 units, no fee, a 14-day stay limit, flush toilets and not much else. The site has a May-October season. Elevation is 6200 feet. Windy Point, a mile farther down the dirt road, has 10 units, no fee, table-bench units, and flush toilets. Season is May-October. Elevation is 6100 feet.

*(Left) At some places along the shoreline of Lake Havasu you can stay in an RV and have your boat almost at the doorstep—the best of both worlds. James Tallon*

**Katherine Landing** is the National Park Service campground on Lake Mohave, just above Davis Dam and about 32 miles west of Kingman off State Route 68. Fee; 30-day stay limit; 173 sites with water, modern restrooms, and table-bench-grill units. Campground is open all year, but the 650-foot elevation makes summer months very warm. The campground is part of a resort that offers boat rentals, a complete marina, motel, store, and cafe. It's just a few steps from the water, so bring your boat.

**Davis Camp,** administered by Mohave County Parks, is 5 miles south of Katherine Landing. Its large, open camping areas and 94-unit recreational vehicle park front almost a mile of Colorado River shoreline. The pull-through units are equipped with water, electricity, and sewage hookups. A dump station, flush toilets and hot showers are available. Open areas at the river's edge accommodate 500 campsites. Fishing and boating are popular. Fee; 14-day stay limit for dry camping; 30-day limit at recreational vehicle park. Open all year.

**Windsor Beach,** an Arizona State Park campground off State Route 95 within the western edge of Lake Havasu City limits, has 132 units and a paved boat launch ramp. Open all year, the campground is at an elevation of 450 feet. Two-week stay limit; fee; water; modern restrooms; hot showers; table-bench units and ramadas. Recreation includes swimming and a system of hiking trails.

**Wild Cow** is a Bureau of Land Management campground 12 miles southeast of Kingman on Hualapai Mountain Road. At an elevation of 6250 feet, the 12-unit site has a May-October season. No fee; 14-day stay limit. Wild Cow's only conveniences are flush toilets and table-bench units.

**Hualapai Mountain Park** is perched atop that mountain range 14 miles south of Kingman. It is part of the Mohave County Parks system. Seventy-four sites in the pines, with water and restrooms; 14-day stay limit. Campground is open all year and access is paved. Eleven sites have recreational vehicle hookups, and there are 14 rustic cabins for rent. Water is turned off during the winter months. Elevation is 6200 feet.

**Lake Havasu** provides extensive boat-access camping. You launch your boat at Cattail Cove, about 15 miles south of Lake Havasu City, then choose any of 170 campsites along the eastern shore of the lake. There are no roads to these sites. They are grouped in twos and threes, sharing a restroom.

Each site has a table-bench unit and a beach for the boat. No water supply. Fee; 14-day stay limit; sites open all year. Elevation is 450 feet, so summer temperatures encourage lots of time in the water.

**Cattail Cove,** in addition to being the launch area for boat campers, has a first-class state park campground. The 40 sites offer water and electric hookups and table-bench units. There are modern restrooms with hot showers. Fee; stay limit, 14 days. Campground is open all year. Access is paved, off State Route 95 about 14 miles south of Lake Havasu City. You camp right on the shore of the lake, with splendid views.

**Buckskin Mountain State Park,** popular with water-skiers and pleasure boaters, is off State Route 95 just south of Parker Dam and about 11 miles north of the town of Parker. Facilities include cabana units at the water's edge, plus a more conventional campground. There are 105 sites, 40 with water and electric hookups. This is an Arizona State Parks system facility. Fee; 14-day stay limit; year-round season. Modern restrooms. Elevation is 420 feet.

**Alamo Lake** is on the Bill Williams River, about 30 miles before it enters the Colorado. Access is 38 paved miles north of Wenden and U.S. Route 60. This Arizona State Park has room for 400 campers. Nineteen sites feature all hookups, and 64 have table-bench-grill units. Modern restrooms; hot showers. Fee; 14-day stay limit; open all year. Elevation is 1250 feet. Much of the camping here is tied to fishing, which tends to be best in spring and early summer. Paved launch ramp; store with camping, fishing, and marine supplies; rental boats.

**Burro Creek** is the Bureau of Land Management's delightful campground just downstream from Burro Creek bridge on U.S. Route 93, 45 miles south of Interstate Route 40 and 55 miles northwest of Wickenburg. About 60 sites; room for more camping in the overflow area. Most campers here come in recreational vehicles; many enjoy the area's abundant rockhounding opportunities. This is desert country, so temperatures are high during the summer, but fall, winter, and spring are very pleasant. Fee; open all year.

# The Navajo-Hopi Reservations

The Navajo Indian Reservation—home of the Navajo Nation, the largest Indian tribe in the United States—surrounds the Hopi Indian Reservation. Together they comprise an area so huge it is somewhat intimidating. Visitors are welcome, including those who linger to camp and explore, but the exotic landscape and the natural reticence of the Indians, can combine to produce a feeling that we are trespassing on a fragile land and a way of life better left undisturbed.

But this is fascinating country, well worth investigating—especially if you take time and have the patience to learn something about the people.

In a sense, these Indian lands can be divided into four areas. First, the stereotypical images of Navajo country: Canyon de Chelly, Monument Valley, flocks of sheep, trading posts, etc. found along the main highways. A second comprises the bulk of the remaining Navajo lands—sagebrush valleys between sandstone buttes—where much of the real life of the Navajo takes place. It is accessible only by back roads and is seldom seen by the casual visitor. The third, and least known, is the Chuska Mountains, north of Window Rock, the Navajo capital. This region surprises visitors with alpine forests and high mountain lakes—far from the stereotype of the Navajo

homeland. The fourth is the Hopi Mesas where a complex ancient culture, vastly different from the Navajo, has thrived continuously for more than a thousand years.

So far camping on the reservations is relatively limited. Primitive camping and picnic areas can be found at a number of places, occasionally offering a ramada, more often just a table and trash barrel near an overlook, ruin, or lake. The Navajo have provided a full-service campground at Monument Valley Tribal Park, and the National Park Service administers two excellent facilities at Canyon de Chelly and Navajo national monuments. Only four other locations on the Navajo reservation qualify as established campgrounds. Although camping is permitted in a number of areas, they are essentially without improvements or services—but the settings are often spectacular. The Hopi Indian Reservation offers four designated campgrounds at the Hopi Cultural Center, Keams Canyon, Oraibi Wash, and Pumpkin Seed Point.

*(Right) The Navajo people are beautiful but reserved; it takes some time to get to know them. J. Peter Mortimer (Below) The campground at Monument Valley Tribal Park is set amidst one of the most photographed areas in the West. James Tallon*

(Above) A canopy of cottonwood trees shades the campground at Canyon de Chelly. Lou DeSerio
(Left) Window Arch in Canyon de Chelly. David Muench
(Below) Navajo horses on the sandy floor of Canyon de Chelly. George McCullough

# The Land of the Long Shadows

## Around the Campfire

Geologists like to say this vast land of dramatic, salmon-hued sandstone spires was once buried 3000 feet beneath ancient seas. Over the next several million years, layer after layer of sediment was deposited, then hardened; this was followed by an uplifting of the land. It's difficult to imagine, but the tops of these mountains and spires were, at one time, at ground level. As the land continued to rise and the sea abated, the forces of wind, rain, and time etched and sculptured the spectacular sandstone monoliths that distinguish Monument Valley.

Anthropologists generally agree that the people we call Navajo came to North America 6000 years ago over a land bridge across the Bering Strait. They go on to say these people drifted down from what is now Canada and began to settle in Monument Valley about 500 years ago.

Scientifically speaking, that's how all this came to be. However, the old Navajo Medicine Man tells it another way. It is usually in winter, when Left Handed Wind howls fiercely across the land, that listeners gather inside the warm confines of a hogan and Storyteller once again recalls the legend of the emergence of Dineh—The People—into the Glittering World.

According to legend, the People progressed through three previous worlds before arriving in this, the Fourth World. First World was black, for there was no light from the heavens. The creatures who inhabited First World had no form and were called Mist People.

In this mythological world, First Man and First Woman were created. Their purpose was to arrange conditions suitable for the Navajo. Unfortunately, there were Evil Beings who quarreled and began casting evil spells upon one another; so First Man and First Woman, along with the Mist People, moved up into the Second or Blue World. Here they found other people and also animals, including badgers, wolves, kit foxes, and cougars. These animals were at war with each other, and to add to the chaos, the Evil Beings from First World also emerged into Second World. Coyote, a cunning but sometimes mischievous creature, persuaded the People to leave the miseries of the Blue World and move to Third World.

The Third World was called Yellow World and had two rivers. One was a female, and ran north and south. The other was male; it ran east and west. First Woman was not happy with Third World and wanted the People to move on to Fourth World. She encouraged Coyote to steal Water Monster's baby, knowing this would anger Water Monster. As expected, Water Monster caused a great flood. All the People and animals climbed up and out of Yellow World, entering the Fourth or Glittering World. Turkey was the last to escape the rising flood waters. At the last moment, the waters touched the tip of Turkey's tail feathers, and that is why to this day the tips of turkey tail feathers are white.

In Fourth World, the deities called Yay-ee-ee instructed the People in how to live in a peaceful way, and First Man and First Woman taught their fellows how to build hogans and to bless them with white and yellow cornmeal along with pollen and powder from prayer sticks. The first hogan was supported by five forked poles: one each on the north, south, and west, and two supporting the doorway, which was always on the east because First Headman, who gave wisdom to the People, lived in that direction.

Day and Night, the Sun, Moon, and stars were created in Fourth World. The four sacred mountains, San Francisco, Navajo, La Plata, and Blanca, were formed from soil carried from Third World.

One day First Man and First Woman found a baby girl. The child grew rapidly into the beautiful Changing Woman, representing nature and the seasons. She became the most beloved of all the Holy People.

Changing Woman mated with the Sun and gave birth to the Twins. Because Fourth World was infested with terrible monsters, Changing Woman feared the Twins would be harmed. She hid them deep underground in a hole she had dug in the hogan. Even their father, the Sun, did not know their whereabouts. One day the Twins discovered another deep hole, where they found Spider Woman. Spider Woman liked the Twins and promised to protect them from the Monsters by teaching them special prayers and chants. The Twins returned to Changing Woman and told her of the great powers given them by Spider Woman. Having no reason now to fear the monsters, Changing Woman and the Twins cast a spell on the huge beasts, turning them to stone.

Today those massive monsters stand frozen in time in Monument Valley. And that is how this beautiful valley and its indestructible people came into being.

## Campfire Recipes

### NAVAJO FRY BREAD

This makes a good lunch treat or an alternative to rolls or ordinary bread at dinnertime. It's important to follow the recipe closely. Although other oil or shortening can be used, the bread tastes best when made the old-fashioned way, with lard.

In a bowl, combine 6 cups unsifted flour, 1 tablespoon salt, 2 tablespoons baking powder, and 1/2 cup instant non-fat dry milk. Add just enough lukewarm water (about 2 1/2 cups) to make a soft dough. Knead thoroughly. Pinch off a ball of dough about the size of a large egg and shape it round and flat, with a small hole in the middle. Work it back and forth from hand to hand, gradually stretching it to a diameter of nine inches. In a frying pan or Dutch oven, have hot melted lard ready at least one inch deep. Fry the round to a light brown on one side; turn, and brown the other. The hole in the middle lets the hot oil bubble up and speeds cooking, so the bread is light and crisp. Drain on a paper towel. Serve plain or with toppings such as jam, honey, or butter. Or sprinkle with powdered sugar and serve as dessert. Best eaten outdoors, beside a cheery fire!

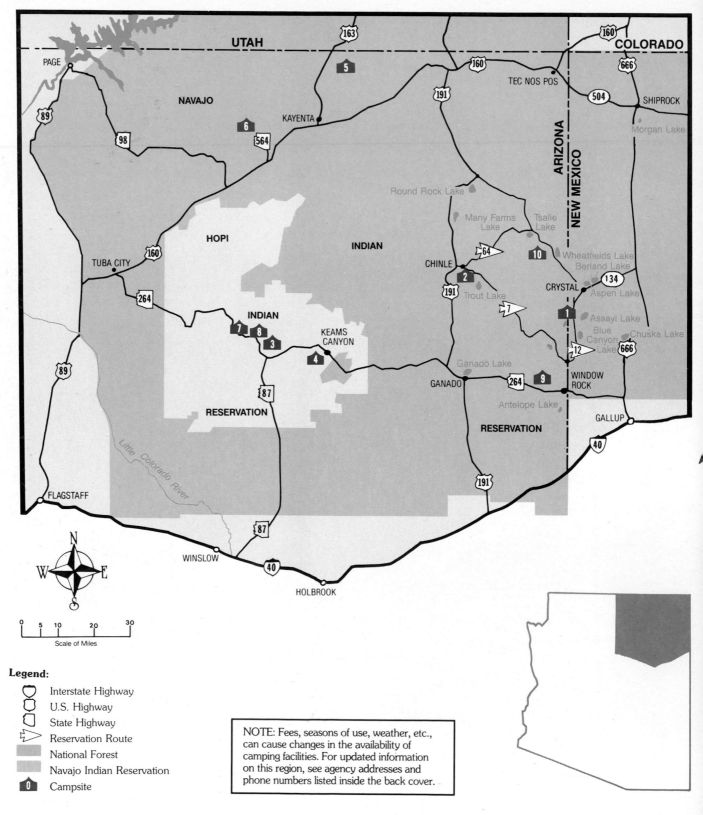

UTAH

COLORADO

PAGE

NAVAJO

KAYENTA

TEC NOS POS

SHIPROCK

Morgan Lake

ARIZONA

NEW MEXICO

Round Rock Lake

Many Farms Lake

Tsalie Lake

HOPI

INDIAN

CHINLE

Wheatfields Lake

Berland Lake

TUBA CITY

Trout Lake

CRYSTAL

Aspen Lake

INDIAN

KEAMS CANYON

Assayi Lake

Blue Canyon Lake

Chuska Lake

Ganado Lake

RESERVATION

GANADO

WINDOW ROCK

Antelope Lake

GALLUP

RESERVATION

FLAGSTAFF

Little Colorado River

WINSLOW

HOLBROOK

Scale of Miles

**Legend:**

Interstate Highway

U.S. Highway

State Highway

Reservation Route

National Forest

Navajo Indian Reservation

Campsite

NOTE: Fees, seasons of use, weather, etc., can cause changes in the availability of camping facilities. For updated information on this region, see agency addresses and phone numbers listed inside the back cover.

# Navajo-Hopi Country Campsites

**Wheatfields Lake** is one of the more popular Navajo campgrounds. Access is easy; a paved road, Navajo Route 12, runs right through the scattered sites. The lake is about 50 miles north of Window Rock. Fishing in the lake is permitted year-round, and the 7200-foot elevation offers pleasant temperatures in summer. No water supply. A small store open all year sells groceries. Fee; 14-day stay limit. About 27 sites; outhouses.

**Summit** campground is in the pines beside State Route 264 a few miles west of Window Rock. No water supply. Fee; 28 sites. Elevation is 7600 feet.

**Assayi Lake** offers 19 sites around a small lake. Campers come every month of the year, though the 8200-foot elevation makes spring, summer, and fall the most comfortable seasons. No water supply. Fee; table-bench units; pit toilets. Access is by way of Navajo Route 12 northeast of Navajo, N.M.

**Mitten View** campground is at the Navajo Tribal Park in Monument Valley. The 100 sites are next to the park headquarters, and the views are outstanding. Elevation here is 5500 feet. Snow is not common, but the campground's season is May to October. Nearby picnic areas are open year-round. Fee; modern restrooms; hot showers. Water spigots, table-bench units, standup grills, ramadas. Dump station for holding tanks. The park is near U. S. Route 163 just south of the Arizona-Utah border.

**Canyon de Chelly** campground is under the jurisdiction of the National Park Service. It's just outside the community of Chinle on Navajo Route 7. The 104 sites are open all year. No fee; 14-day stay limit. Campground is shaded by cottonwood trees. Modern restrooms; water spigots convenient to all sites. Dump station available. You're about a half-mile from the spectacular canyon itself and just down the hill from the Park Service visitor center. A lodge is nearby, and canyon tours can be arranged there. Campground may fill on holidays, but usually has spaces available otherwise.

The campground at **Navajo National Monument** is also a Park Service facility. It has 30 sites, modern restrooms, water throughout the campground, and is open from May 15 to October 15. Table-bench-grill units are located in a forest of juniper and pine at an elevation of 7300 feet. No fee; 7-day stay limit. Visitor center presents displays and films on the Anasazi culture that flourished here before the coming of the Navajo. Access road is State Route 564, which leaves U.S. Route 160 southwest of Kayenta.

**Keams Canyon** is a 5-unit campground among the cottonwood trees in its namesake canyon. There are table-bench units and fire pits, but no water, no facilities, no stay limit, and no fee. During summer months kachina dance ceremonies are often held at Hopi villages within easy driving distance, so make local inquiries. Keams Canyon Trading Post, restaurant, and motel are nearby. Elevation is 5500 feet; open all year.

**Hopi Cultural Center** is set on top of Second Mesa. This 5-unit camping area is next door to the Cultural Center, with its fine motel, restaurant, and museum. The Hopi Arts and Crafts Guild, with a vast selection of pottery, basketry, jewelry, and weavings, is within walking distance. There are fire pits and table-bench units, but no water, no facilities, no stay limit, and no fee. Elevation is 6000 feet; open all year.

**Oraibi Wash** sets on a sandy bench on the east side of Oraibi Wash. This 3-unit site has fire pits, table-bench units, and outhouses, but nothing else. No fee, no stay limit, open all year. Night skies always seem clearer and the stars more abundant in Hopiland.

**Pumpkin Seed Point** is situated on a rocky promontory just east of the village of Oraibi. This 3-unit campground presents a spectacular mesa-top view of the surrounding country, particularly at dawn and dusk. Fire pits, table-bench units, no stay limit, no fee, and no facilities. Open all year.

| | RECREATION SITE NAME | APPROX. ELEV. | SEASONS OF USE | DAYS-LIMITS | FEE | NO. OF UNITS | SAFE WATER | 16 FT. RV LIMIT | WASTE DISP. | BOATING | FISHING |
|---|---|---|---|---|---|---|---|---|---|---|---|
| 1 | ASSAYI LAKE | 8200 | All Yr. | 14 | X | 19 | | X | | X | X |
| 2 | CANYON DE CHELLY | 5500 | All Yr. | 14 | | 104 | X | | X | | |
| 3 | HOPI CULTURAL CENTER | 6000 | All Yr. | none | | 5 | | | | | |
| 4 | KEAMS CANYON | 5500 | All Yr. | none | | 5 | | | | | |
| 5 | MITTEN VIEW | 5500 | May Oct. | 14 | X | 100 | X | | X | | |
| 6 | NAVAJO NAT. MONUMENT | 7300 | May Oct. | 7 | | 30 | X | | X | | |
| 7 | ORAIBI WASH | | All Yr. | none | | 3 | | | | | |
| 8 | PUMPKIN SEED POINT | | All Yr. | none | | 3 | | | | | |
| 9 | SUMMIT | 7600 | All Yr. | 14 | X | 28 | | X | | | |
| 10 | WHEATFIELDS LAKE | 7200 | All Yr. | 14 | X | 27 | | X | | X | X |

# North Central Arizona

When the names roll off the tongue they are Arizona names, made in the West, as true as the cry of the coyote and the mountain named for old Bill Williams. Hear them now: Dead Horse Ranch, Horsethief Basin, Happy Jack, Skull Valley, Banjo Bill, Canyon Diablo. Or Dogtown, Bumble Bee, Blowout Mountain, and Deadmans Pocket.

They come from the heart of Arizona, the country that contains the towns of Flagstaff, Williams, Prescott, Cottonwood, Camp Verde, and Sedona—and some of the best camping in the state.

History keeps a light guiding hand on your elbow no matter where you go in this region. If you camp along West Clear Creek, a few miles east of Camp Verde, for example, you're on the road traveled by Army

troops who left the fort to pursue Apache renegades a century ago. And when Amos Adams camped outside Prescott in August, 1875, he couldn't have parked his wagon too far from the present-day White Spar campground. Adams' diary notes that the day after he arrived in the area, after a four-month journey from Missouri, he took "a No. 1 scrub in the creek"; then he and a friend got dressed up and went into Prescott. "A very pretty place but most stores are saloons." The following day's entry informs us he "got up with a powerful headache." He was able to "eat but little breakfast," and got sick soon after.

Or you might camp south of Flagstaff, maybe even over the Fourth of July weekend, and wonder which of the stories about the town's naming is really true. Was a tall pine tree stripped of its branches to serve as a staff for the flag on some glorious Fourth in the past?

It is the pine trees and cool summer temperatures that attract most campers to north central Arizona. The Prescott, Kaibab, and Coconino national forests are the major landlords. They offer some campgrounds that are open year-round but the April-October period is the most popular with visitors, and that's when the majority of the facilities are in operation. Campgrounds in both the Flagstaff and Prescott areas are close enough to metropolitan Phoenix to get tremendous pressure. Some super-popular spots, like Lynx Lake at Prescott, Pine Grove south of Flagstaff, and almost any campground in Oak Creek Canyon, are always full during the summer months. As soon as one camper begins to pack up to leave, another parks nearby and waits for the spot. It's always a good idea to have an alternative campground or two in mind, in case your first choice is completely full and looks as if it will stay that way.

Other campgrounds tend to empty and fill again almost daily, as cross-country travelers use them for overnight stops. Bonito campground, across the road from the visitor center at Sunset Crater National Monument north of Flagstaff, is a good example. It is full of vacationers every night, but the great majority move on next morning and it's usually easy to find an open site from midmorning to midafternoon. And—indicating the great popularity of the place with foreign visitors—you're likely to hear conversations in half a dozen languages, if you take an after-supper walk around the campground.

This region is a great favorite with Arizona families. Thousands of youngsters spent their first night under canvas somewhere in this wonderful area, overindulged in toasted marshmallows, and learned the old songs around evening campfires. Many of those camping trips also yielded a first trout or the first sight of antelope, deer, elk, or the tassel-eared squirrels that frequent the ponderosas. Surely the stuff of many more memories awaits your next visit.

*(Above left) Chasing northern pike on Lower Lake Mary.* Tom Bean
*(Right) Oak Creek's campgrounds are among the most popular in Arizona during the summer months. The surroundings are cool and green, and there's a chance at rainbow trout.* James Tallon

(Above) This is the scene desert dwellers dream about between trips to the high pine country. James Tallon
(Right) Lockett Meadow in the inner basin of the San Francisco peaks, with huge groves of aspen trees spilling down the mountainside. Tom Danielson

(Top) Children love camping the most.
J. Peter Mortimer
(Above) A small boat is plenty big enough for Lynx Lake,
especially when both crew members paddle. Dick Dietrich
(Right) Hot coffee and a Coleman lantern; camping's not
camping without them. James Tallon

# Around the Campfire: The Heart of Arizona

Back in 1540, Francisco Vasquez de Coronado led an expedition across Arizona in search of the mythical Seven Cities of Gold. The Spanish adventurers followed a forbidding path along waterless desert valleys, through twisting, boulder-choked canyons, and across brawny mountain ranges. They came up empty in their quest for fortune, but found, in the words of their chronicler, "a good place to search." Old Mother Nature's rough hands couldn't have created a better place on this earth to hide a treasure than right here in Arizona. It's also a good place to lose one, and there are more lost mines in the heart of Arizona than politicians have plans.

Most of these mysterious mines have a history of being found, then lost again. The stories stay pretty much the same: Prospector finds rich treasure, thinks he has memorized the exact spot, and leaves. Upon his return, his mind starts playing tricks on him, and he can't relocate the elusive strike.

Back in the 1870s, a pair of itinerant sourdoughs followed a Yavapai Indian into the narrow canyons east of today's Black Canyon City. Earlier, in Phoenix, they had seen him pay for his supplies with a handful of nuggets and were determined to find the Indian's mine and claim the riches for themselves. Somewhere along the Agua Fria they lost him, and, while trying to pick up his trail, they stumbled upon a granite outcropping laced with pure gold.

The two men, whose names were Brown and Davies, quickly filled their saddle-bags with some $80,000 worth of rich ore and started to leave the narrow canyon. Just then a war party of Yavapais showed up and opened fire. Davies toppled from his saddle, mortally wounded. Brown, who was bringing up the rear, dove behind a huge boulder and prepared to make a last stand. Four well-placed shots dispatched the riders of three ponies and wounded a fourth warrior. Retrieving their injured comrade, the Indians rode away. Brown hid out in a manzanita thicket until it was safe to emerge, then buried his bags of ore on the east bank of an arroyo. He pocketed one ore specimen, took a long look around to make sure of his bearings, and—just to make sure he could relocate the site—lodged his prospector's pick in the side of an old saguaro.

Brown escaped from the canyon and made his way to California. In San Francisco he had the specimen assayed. The report valued the gold ore at $84,000 to the ton.

Brown waited for the Indian wars to end before returning to Arizona. By this time he was 80 years old. On his way to the Agua Fria River country he took sick and was placed in a hospital. On his death bed the old prospector revealed, for the first time, the story of his "Lost Pick Mine." I reckon he figured some other old sourdough deserved to find it.

Well, none ever did. A Mexican sheepherder did claim he'd seen a saguaro with a pick stuck in its hide, but he couldn't recollect exactly where it was.

Most folks believe all the lost Spanish treasures lie south of the Gila River, but at least one is lost somewhere in the arroyos around central Arizona's Sycamore Canyon. Sometime during the 1760s, a small party prospecting in the Verde Valley found a rich gold vein somewhere between today's Sedona and Perkinsville. The Spanish miners didn't know it at the time, but their every move was being watched by Tonto Apaches. As the party prepared to move out, the warriors swarmed through the camp. Three were killed instantly; a fourth, his body punctured with arrows, was dragged away to be put to death slowly over the hot coals of a campfire. Two other miners were able to make a getaway. After two weeks of hard traveling, the two straggled into the presidio at Tubac, on the Santa Cruz River in southern Arizona.

Nothing on God's earth could make the two survivors return to the land of the Tonto Apaches, but they did provide a map for anyone brave or foolhardy enough to try. The lost mine was located in a red cliff overlooking a hard-to-find box canyon. Part of the cliff looks like an Apache warrior turned sideways. The cheekbones are high, with a rather large nose. Just beneath the nose is the lost gold mine.

The lost mine in Sycamore Canyon has never been found. Every once in a while, someone claims to have stumbled upon some adobe ruins or the crumbling remains of an old arrastra; but as with other lost mines scattered around Arizona, the treasure's whereabouts remains a secret of the silent canyons and brooding mountains.

Not all of Arizona's lost treasures are mines. Somewhere near Happy Jack, a small lumber town between Flagstaff and Clints Well, lies a quarter million dollars in gold coin taken during a stage robbery.

Back in 1879, a stagecoach, carrying a secret shipment of gold from Santa Fe to Prescott, was waylaid at the old stage station at Pine Springs. The only passenger was killed, but the driver, Mose Stacey, was able to get away. Stacey rode into Flagstaff and rounded up a posse. The hard-riding men rode into Pine Springs and surrounded the station, trapping the four desperadoes inside. After an all-night siege, the lawmen set fire to the building. The bandits rushed from the burning station with pistols blazing. Sharpshooters placed near the entrance picked them off one by one.

Well, dead men tell no tales. The possemen were unable to find the gold in the charred ruins. It was calculated that the outlaws had less than an hour to cache the three boxes of coins. Searchers scoured the area around the station to no avail. The gold's still out there somewhere.

Loot from another stage robbery remains lost somewhere near Canyon Diablo, east of Flagstaff.

On May 10, 1881, two mailbags containing $125,000 in gold and silver bars were taken from the boot of the Canyon Diablo-Flagstaff stage. Since the robbery involved the U.S. Mail, federal troops joined a large posse in pursuit of the outlaws. Trackers picked up the hoofprints of five horses and followed them into the high country around Veit Spring.

The troopers caught up with the desperadoes at the spring. The bandits chose to shoot it out, and in a furious exchange of gunfire, all five were killed. But the "Dead Outlaws' Loot" was never recovered.

Then one day in 1913, "Short Jimmy" McGuire popped into a Flagstaff saloon and dropped a handful of gold coins on the bar. He ordered the barkeeper to "set up drinks fer everyone." Short Jimmy, a character of local renown, claimed he'd located the "Dead Outlaws' Loot" near the spring using a willow fork similar to the ones carried by water witchers. By this time, a huge crowd of well-wishers had gathered to help him celebrate. McGuire, basking in the glory of his new-found wealth and notoriety, had downed his fourth shot of whiskey when he keeled over dead of a heart attack.

A short lived but futile gold rush to Veit Spring followed. Gold-seekers found Short Jimmy's camp but not the rest of the treasure. Like most of Arizona's lost mines and treasures, the "Dead Outlaws' Loot" lies waiting to be found by some lucky modern-day argonaut.

# Campfire Recipes

### BREAKFAST DELIGHT

The easy way: Cut a two-inch hole in the center of a slice of bread; butter both sides of the slice and place on a hot skillet. Drop a dot of butter in the hole, then break an egg there. Put a slice of cheese over the egg and place several strips of precooked bacon over the top. Cover and cook quickly.

### MINI-PIZZAS

Use an English muffin as the pizza base. Add pizza sauce (canned) and slices of pepperoni and cheese. Heat on campfire grill or in a covered skillet.

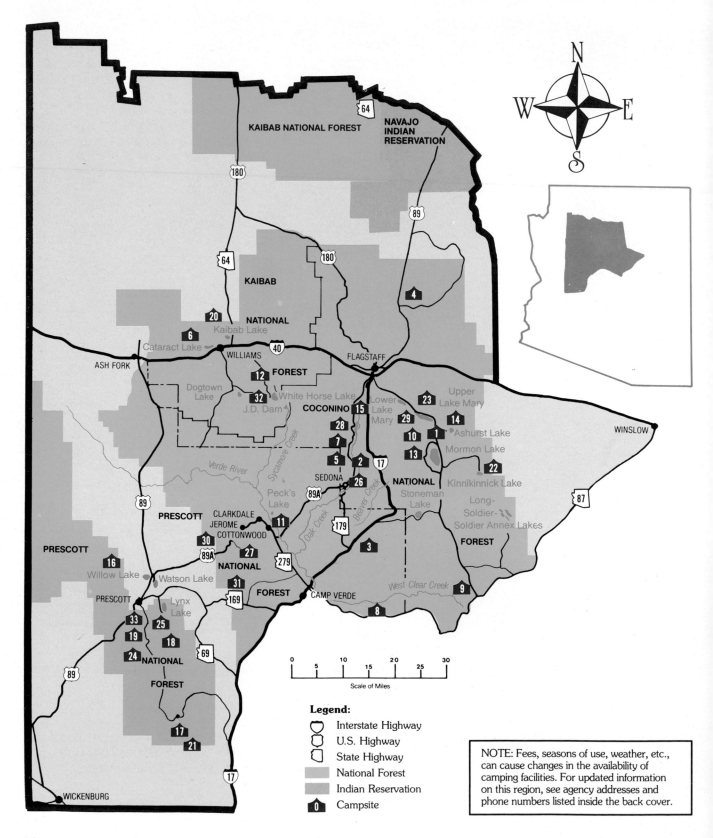

N
W E
S

KAIBAB NATIONAL FOREST

NAVAJO
INDIAN
RESERVATION

64

180

KAIBAB

64

NATIONAL

4

20
Kaibab Lake

6
Cataract Lake

ASH FORK

WILLIAMS

40

FLAGSTAFF

12 FOREST

Upper
Lake Mary

23

Dogtown
Lake

32

White Horse Lake

COCONINO

15

Lower
Lake
Mary

29

14 Ashurst Lake

J.D. Dam

28

10 1

WINSLOW

7

13 Mormon Lake

5

Verde River

Sycamore Creek

2

17

22 Kinnikinnick Lake

SEDONA

26

NATIONAL

87

Peck's
Lake

89A

Stoneman
Lake

Long-
Soldier-
Soldier Annex Lakes

PRESCOTT

CLARKDALE
JEROME

11

Oak Creek

Beaver Creek

FOREST

30 COTTONWOOD

89A

27

179

3

PRESCOTT

16

NATIONAL

279

Willow Lake

Watson Lake

West Clear Creek

9

31

FOREST

CAMP VERDE

Prescott

Lynx
Lake

169

8

33

25

19

18

24 NATIONAL

69

89

FOREST

17

21

17

WICKENBURG

0    5    10    15    20    25    30
Scale of Miles

Legend:
Interstate Highway
U.S. Highway
State Highway
National Forest
Indian Reservation
0    Campsite

NOTE: Fees, seasons of use, weather, etc.,
can cause changes in the availability of
camping facilities. For updated information
on this region, see agency addresses and
phone numbers listed inside the back cover.

# North Central Arizona Campsites

**Clints Well** is near the junction of State Route 87 and the Mormon Lake road to Flagstaff. There are only 7 improved campsites, but there's room among the tall pines for several self-contained recreational vehicles. There's no water and thus no fee, but a store and service station are nearby. Open May-November, the stay limit, 14 days. The original spring, not far from the campground, was named for Clint Wingfield, whose family still has a ranch in the area.

**Double Springs** is on the western shore of Mormon Lake. The lake is sometimes vast but shallow, sometimes a reedy marsh. The 16-unit campground is beside Forest Road 90, about 30 miles south of Flagstaff. It is open from May to September. Elevation is 7000 feet, and you'll find the sites delightfully shaded by pines. Fee; water; table-bench units, fire rings, restrooms. Trailers over 16 feet are discouraged.

**Dairy Springs** has the same sort of setup as Double Springs, but it's about a mile closer to Flagstaff. There are 27 sites here; season is May-September. Nice northern pike in the lake, too!

**Kinnikinnick Lake** takes its name from the Indian word for a shrub in the bearberry family, which grows in this vicinity. The campground is on the shore of the lake. There are only 14 sites, but there's ample room for additional self-contained recreational vehicles. No potable water; no fee. Season is May-September. Kinnikinnick is southeast of Mormon Lake, about 9 miles via rough roads.

**Ashurst Lake** is a 25-unit campground situated among junipers and pines at the edge of a popular trout lake, about 20 miles south of Flagstaff. Season is May to September. Fee; 7-day stay limit. Paved access is via Forest Road 82E, which turns east from the

| | RECREATION SITE NAME | APPROX. ELEV. | SEASONS OF USE | DAYS-LIMITS | FEE | NO. OF UNITS | SAFE WATER | 16 FT. RV LIMIT | WASTE DISP. | BOATING | FISHING |
|---|---|---|---|---|---|---|---|---|---|---|---|
| 1 | ASHURST LAKE | 7100 | May Sep. | 7 | X | 25 | X | | | X | X |
| 2 | BANJO BILL | 5000 | May Sep. | 3 | X | 8 | | X | | | X |
| 3 | BEAVER CREEK | 3800 | All Yr. | 7 | X | 13 | X | | | | X |
| 4 | BONITO* | 6900 | Apr. Oct. | 14 | X | 44 | X | | | | |
| 5 | BOOTLEGGER | 5200 | May Sep. | 3 | X | 10 | | | | | X |
| 6 | CATARACT LAKE* | 6800 | May Oct | 14 | X | 18 | X | X | X | X | X |
| 7 | CAVE SPRINGS | 5400 | May Sep. | 7 | X | 78 | X | | | | X |
| 8 | CLEAR CREEK* | 3200 | All Yr. | 7 | X | 18 | X | | | | X |
| 9 | CLINTS WELL | 7000 | May Nov. | 14 | | 7 | | | | | |
| 10 | DAIRY SPRINGS | 7000 | May Sep. | 14 | X | 27 | X | | | X | X |
| 11 | DEAD HORSE RANCH St. Pk. | 3300 | All Yr. | 14 | X | 45 | X | | X | | X |
| 12 | DOGTOWN RESERVOIR | 7000 | May Nov. | 14 | X | 60 | X | | X | X | X |
| 13 | DOUBLE SPRINGS | 7000 | May Sep. | 14 | X | 16 | X | | | | |
| 14 | FORKED PINE | 7000 | May Sep. | 7 | X | 33 | X | | | X | X |
| 15 | FORT TUTHILL | 7000 | May Sep. | 14 | X | 80 | X | | X | | |
| 16 | GRANITE BASIN | 5600 | All Yr. | 14 | | 18 | | | | X | X |
| 17 | HAZLETT HOLLOW | 6000 | May Nov. | 14 | | 15 | X | | | | X |
| 18 | HILLTOP | 6000 | May Sep. | 7 | X | 38 | X | | | X | X |
| 19 | INDIAN CREEK | 5800 | May Sep. | 14 | | 27 | | | | | |
| 20 | KAIBAB LAKE* | 6800 | May Oct. | 14 | X | 60 | X | | X | X | X |
| 21 | KENTUCK SPRINGS | 6000 | May Nov. | 14 | | 15 | | | | | X |
| 22 | KINNIKINNICK LAKE | 7000 | May Sep. | 14 | | 14 | | | | X | X |
| 23 | LAKEVIEW | 7000 | May Sep. | 7 | X | 30 | X | X | | X | X |
| 24 | LOWER WOLF CREEK | 6000 | May Nov. | 14 | | 20 | | | | | |
| 25 | LYNX LAKE | 5500 | Mar. Nov. | 7 | X | 39 | X | | | X | X |
| 26 | MANZANITA* | 4800 | May Sep. | 3 | X | 19 | X | X | X | | |
| 27 | MINGUS MTN. | 7600 | May Oct. | 14 | | 24 | | | | | |
| 28 | PINE FLAT | 5100 | May Oct. | 7 | X | 59 | X | | | | X |
| 29 | PINE GROVE | 7000 | May Sep. | 7 | X | 46 | X | | X | X | X |
| 30 | POTATO PATCH | 6500 | May Oct. | 14 | | 14 | | | | | |
| 31 | POWELL SPRINGS | 5300 | All Yr. | 14 | | 10 | X | X | | | |
| 32 | WHITE HORSE LAKE* | 7000 | May Oct. | 14 | | 85 | X | | | X | X |
| 33 | WHITE SPAR | 5700 | May Sep. | 14 | X | 62 | X | | | | |

* Sites with handicapped facilities.

paved Mormon Lake road about a mile south of the upper end of Upper Lake Mary. Drinking water, plus the usual camping amenities.

**Forked Pine** campground is also at Ashurst Lake. Turn left at the parking lot-launch ramp and follow the road around the northern end of the lake to the 33 sites. Drinking water; fee; 7-day stay limit. Season is May to September. The 7000-foot elevation is refreshingly cool, and the lake is always good for some rainbow trout.

**Pine Grove** is in the tall pines of Coconino National Forest near the southern end of Upper Lake Mary, about 19 miles south of Flagstaff. This is one of the nicer U. S. Forest Service campgrounds in the state. The 46 sites are laid out in loops, with ample room between camps and a good mixture of back-in and pull-through parking. Modern restrooms; table-bench units; user fee; 7-day stay limit. The campground traditionally opens on Memorial Day weekend and closes after Labor Day.

**Fort Tuthill**, a Coconino County Park south of Flagstaff at Interstate 17 and Exit 337, is ideal for those who enjoy organized recreation. The 80-unit campground has a large park 300 yards to the east with facilities for softball, volleyball, racquetball, tennis, and horseshoes, and a large picnic area with ramadas. Ten units have water and sewer hookups; 20 are pull through. Fee; modern restroom and shower building; dump station. Group camping area accommodates 100. Two-week stay limit. Season is May-September.

**Lakeview**, 16 miles south of Flagstaff on the Mormon Lake road, is aptly named. Located on a pine-studded hillside, this delightful campground's 30 sites all have a view of Upper Lake Mary. The access road zigzags up the hill, so motor homes and vehicles pulling trailers are not allowed. Campsites are arranged on wide benches, and pickup campers and tents are much used. Drinking water; 7-day stay limit. Season is May-September.

**Bonito** is at Sunset Crater National Monument. If the moon had pine trees, campgrounds there would look like this. Forty-four sites are located off the entrance road to the crater, about 18 miles northeast of Flagstaff. Open April to October. Operated by the U.S. Forest Service, the campground is opposite Sunset Crater visitor center. User fee; modern restrooms and the usual amenities. There are special sites for handicapped campers. Sleep well: it's been more than 900 years since Sunset Crater erupted.

**Kaibab Lake** campground is in Kaibab National Forest. Its 60 sites are open from May to October. User fee; 14-day stay limit. The campground has a water supply, and some of the sites and restrooms are equipped for the handicapped. The lake is nearby, and trout fishing is very popular. Kaibab Lake is about 2 miles east of Williams on Interstate Route 40, then a mile north on State Route 64, the highway to the Grand Canyon.

**Cataract Lake** is small and does not have a cataract, but the pleasant campground of the same name has 18 sites, and all have a lake view. Fee; 14-day stay limit. Season is May to October. There are trout in the lake, and the town of Williams is just a mile east on Interstate Route 40.

**White Horse Lake**, so the story goes, was named when a surveying crew saw a white horse in the meadow that now holds this lake and campground. Kaibab National Forest has installed 85 sites among the tall pines that surround the lake. Fee; 14-day stay limit; a May-October season. Small store; rental boats. White Horse is about 20 miles south and east of Williams via Forest roads 110 and 109. Some sites are for the handicapped.

**Dogtown Reservoir** has 60 sites on the shore of a lake that covers what used to be a colony of prairie dogs. Water; fee; 14-day stay limit. Season is May-November. Dogtown Reservoir is 6 miles south and east of Williams via Forest Road 140.

**Manzanita** is one of 5 Coconino National Forest campgrounds in Oak Creek Canyon. If you're heading north along the creek out of Sedona, Manzanita is the first. It has 19 sites. User fee; stay limit, 3 days only. Space is limited on the little bench beside the water, so trailers are not allowed. Season is Memorial Day through Labor Day. Access is via U.S. Route 89-A, about 6 miles north of Sedona.

**Banjo Bill** is 8 miles north of Sedona. There are just 8 sites here. Fee; 3-day stay limit; May-September season. Trailers to 16 feet only.

**Bootlegger**, 9 miles north of Sedona, has 10 sites. No drinking water. Fee; 3-day stay limit; May-September season. Shade from the beautiful trees that gave Oak Creek its name.

**Cave Springs** is the canyon's largest campground, with 78 sites in a thickly wooded area about 12 miles north of Sedona and a half-mile west of the highway. A paved road leads to the campground. There is water; a user fee; 7-day stay limit; Memorial Day-Labor Day season. Trailers and motor homes permitted, if not too large.

**Pine Flat** is the last of the Oak Creek campgrounds. Located 14 miles north of Sedona, this one has 59 sites spread in the pines along the creek. Water; fee; 7-day stay limit. The season opens before the other camps in May but lasts till October. The canyon is narrow and deep here, so it may be several hours after the sun rises before its rays touch the campground.

**Clear Creek** is 7 paved miles east of Camp Verde, near West Clear Creek. This appealing 18-site campground is laid out in a huge grove of sycamore trees. Fee; stay limit, 7 days. Season is all year.

**Beaver Creek** has 13 sites. Trout are stocked here in the cool spring and early summer months, but because the elevation is only 3800 feet, it can get warm on summer days. Potable water; fee; 7-day stay limit; open all year. Access is by gravel road 3 miles east of the Sedona-Rimrock interchange on Interstate Route 17.

**Dead Horse Ranch State Park** is near the Verde Valley community of Cottonwood. Water and electric hookups; modern restrooms; hot showers; dump station. Fee; 14-day stay limit; open year-round, but fall, winter, and spring months are the most comfortable. The Verde River runs nearby.

**Potato Patch** is perched on the flank of Mingus Mountain, high above the Verde Valley and about 7 miles up the hill via U.S. Route 89-A from the lively "ghost town" of Jerome. There are 14 sites. No water; no fee. Stay limit is 14 days; the season is May to October.

**Mingus Mountain** campground is reached via Forest Road 104, which makes its unpaved, twisting way for about 2.5 miles from U.S. Route 89-A to the 24 unit destination. Don't try to take a large motor home or a trailer of more than 20 feet on this road. No water; no fee; 14-day stay limit, and a May-October season. One of the sites is on the edge of the mountain, and 100-mile views of the Verde Valley are right out the tent flap — quilt patches of farmland by day, twinkling lights at night. A nearby group site of 9 units can be reserved.

**Powell Springs** is at the foot of Mingus Mountain, about 13 miles northeast of Dewey via State Route 169 and Forest Road 372. The 10 sites are at 5300 feet elevation and open all year. Drinking water; no fee; 14-day stay limit. Powell Springs is restricted to

trailers shorter than 22 feet.

**Granite Basin** has 18 sites in the rolling, granite-studded countryside about 9 miles northwest of Prescott via Iron Springs Road and Forest Road 374. No drinking water; no fee; 14-day stay limit. Open all year.

**White Spar** campground is 3 miles south of Prescott on the road of the same name, also known as U.S. Route 89. There are 62 sites in a grove of pines. Fee; 14-day stay limit. The usual season is May-September, but part of the campground remains open all year. No water is available after temperatures drop below freezing. Elevation is 5700 feet.

**Indian Creek** campground has 27 widely separated sites along the trickle of water named Indian Creek. There is lots of room for trailers and motor homes. No drinking water; no fee; 14-day stay limit. Open from May to September. Access is via Wolf Creek-Groom Creek Road, off U.S. Route 89 about 5 miles south of Prescott.

**Lower Wolf Creek** has 20 campsites, a 14-day stay limit, no water, no fee, and no wolves. Access is via Senator Highway and Groom Creek Road about 9 miles south of Prescott. Season is May-November. **Upper Wolf Creek**, a group site with 21 units, can be reserved.

**Lynx Lake** has modern restrooms on one loop of this popular Prescott National Forest campground. User fee; 7-day stay limit; March-November season. There are 39 sites. One of the closest pine-country campgrounds to the Phoenix area, it's difficult to find an open spot here during summer months. It is 7 miles southeast of Prescott via State Route 69 and paved Forest Road 197.

**Hilltop**, a mile south of the Lynx Lake campground, has 38 sites. It is designed for trailers and recreational vehicles, but is open to other camping modes as well. User fee; 7-day stay limit; May-September season.

**Hazlett Hollow** is 7 bumpy miles southeast of Crown King on Forest Road 52. You have to want to get to this 15-site campground. Water; no fee; 14-day stay limit. Season is May-November.

**Kentuck Springs** is just a mile further down the road from Hazlett Hollow. There are 15 sites here, with a 14-day stay limit, and a May-November season. No water; no fees; and not much company.

# The Mogollon Rim

Arizona campers have been drawn admiringly to the Mogollon Rim for more than a century. The dramatic escarpment (its name is pronounced "Muggy-own") was formed when a portion of the earth's crust shifted, millions of years ago. The resulting escarpment actually runs across several hundred miles of Arizona's midsection; but nowhere is it more splendidly evident, more awesome, or more forbidding than in the forty-mile section north and east of Payson, where its sheer cliffs reach more than a thousand feet high, dividing the pine and juniper country below the Rim from the forests of spruce and fir atop the plateau.

This wild and rugged area was named for Juan Ignacio Flores Mogollon. From 1712 to 1715 he was Spanish governor of the lands that would become Arizona and New Mexico. Señor Mogollon spent most of his time in the palace at Santa Fe, and never saw the sweeping views from the edge of the grand prank of nature that bears his name.

This is a region of tall, deep, quiet forests, both above and below the Rim. Beaver trappers worked the streams here in the early 1800s. A generation later, sheep and cattle ranchers moved in and a few roads appeared, generally following old Indian trails. Army troops established a dim wagon route from Fort Verde to Fort Apache that differed little from the course across the top of the Rim that campers take today, although now the way is much wider and smoother. The deep canyons that run northward from the edge of the Rim, gathering water for the Little Colorado River, were hiding places for renegades who bolted from the San Carlos and Verde reservations, raided ranches and wagon trains, then disappeared into the high country.

Zane Grey liked to disappear here, too, to escape the attention he garnered as one of the world's best-selling authors and to gather new ideas, new locales, and new characters for the dozen novels he would write with Arizona backgrounds. And so, from the early part of the century to the late 1920s, he came here to hunt and fish and camp.

Now desert dwellers are the ones who disappear each summer, seeking the coolness of the 7500-foot elevations, filling campgrounds on the shores of lakes and streams or in the groves of pines. Tonto National Forest is in charge of the land below the Rim; the Coconino and Apache-Sitgreaves forests divide the wooded plateau above. Between them they guarantee an almost complete absence of "No Trespassing" signs. Dozens of old logging roads wind along the ridgetops, leading to hundreds of shady dells where you can be king of the woods for a day or a week.

This is summer country. Most of the campgrounds open in May and close in September. Mogollon Rim means trees and cool camping beneath them: pine and oak, fir and spruce, quaking aspen, alligator juniper, maple and the sycamore, locust and walnut and ash. The Rim means elk feeding in a meadow at dawn; a tassel-eared squirrel sending signals with its white tail from the limb of a great ponderosa pine; the distinctive smell of limestone canyon walls; a patch of ripe raspberries no one else knows about.

That's camping in the Rim country.

*(Above left) Spooky tales and outrageous jokes around the campfire; for many it is the best part of the camping day. George McCullough*
*(Right) A view from the edge of the Mogollon Rim, that great escarpment that runs across Arizona's midsection. It is both a place and a lazy, relaxed state of mind. Dick Dietrich*

*(Right) Sunflowers decorate the meadow at one of the Rim's smallest and loveliest campgrounds, Kehl Springs. Jerry Sieve*
*(Below) Today's recreation is tomorrow's fond memory. Fred Griffin*
*(Bottom) Most trout from Rim lakes are pan-sized, but occasionally a lunker comes along, like this rainbow from Willow Springs Lake. Lewis G. Davis*

*A fleet of canoes on the broad, blue bosom of Knoll Lake.
They could be headed for the upper end of the lake and
an overnight campout.* James Tallon

# Mogollon Monikers

Ever since man first set foot in this rugged piece of terrain known as Arizona, he has felt compelled to brand everything with a name. Inspiration for these place names came from a variety of sources—some quite obvious. When Mormon pioneers decided to settle near a large stand of ponderosa pines, they simply named their community Pine. Another group settled in a small valley where they found wild berries growing in abundance and decided to name their town Strawberry. Henry Clifton, a member of an early Indian-fighting militia, claimed that in 1864 the place was known as Wah-Poo-Eta for a prominent Tonto Apache chief better known to whites as Big Rump. The most obvious place name in Mogollon Rim country was bestowed when a group of settlers pulled into a little green valley and promptly named it Little Green Valley.

Sometimes names get changed in the process. Star Valley was named for old John Starr, who moved to Arizona from Oregon with his Indian wife in 1877. Apparently the extra "r" got lost somewhere along the way. That's not nearly as bad as what happened to Henry Mortimore Coane over in the Verde Valley. His application to Washington to establish a post office was misread. The name Coaneville was requested, but some bureaucrat scribbled in "Cornville", and that's what it is today.

I reckon people have been the source for most of the place names in the Rim country. The name Mogollon is not Indian as often presumed, but comes from Juan Ignacio Flores Mogollon, governor of the Spanish province of New Mexico in the early 1700s.

Payson, the largest town in these parts, was named for Senator Louis Payson, who helped establish a post office here in 1884. Earlier names included Long Valley, Big Valley, Green Valley, and Union Park. In 1882 the first building, a stockade, was created. This historic site was located on what is today the fifth green of the Payson golf course.

Houston Mesa was named for Sam and Andrew Houston, who ran cattle here in the 1880s. Sam was killed in a freak accident. He got off his horse to tighten the cinch and flipped the stirrup over the saddle. His pistol was in a holster tied to the saddle horn, and the stirrup struck the hammer, causing it to discharge. The bullet hit Sam in the leg, and he bled to death before he could get to a doctor.

During the early 1880s, Isadore Christopher located the CI Ranch on the creek that bears his name. The ranch became the target of frequent attacks by Apaches. The war parties kept burning his place, but the stubborn rancher continued to rebuild. One day in 1882, he killed a large bear and nailed the hide on the side of his barn to dry. He was out hunting a few days later when a band of marauding Apaches rode in and set fire to the place. Army troops arrived on the scene and drove off the war party. When the soldiers saw that bearhide among the charred ruins of the barn, they thought it was poor old Christopher. Legend has it they held a solemn funeral and buried the bearskin. It was such a touching occasion Christopher hated to have to break the news that his death, like Mark Twain's, was a bit exaggerated.

One of the most important military roads during the Apache wars was the Crook Trail along the Mogollon Rim from Fort Apache to Camp Verde. The road was used primarily in the 1870s before the arrival of the railroad, but wagon ruts, and blaze marks on the ancient pine trees, are still visible in some sections today.

Martha Summerhayes, a young army bride, rode in an ambulance-supply wagon over that rough and sometimes precipitous trail in 1874. Martha had a proper New England upbringing and found it hard to adjust to the coarse language used by the teamsters to coax their animals up the steep grades. I'll let her tell it: "Each mule got its share of dreadful curses. I had never heard or conceived of any oaths such as those. They made my blood fairly curdle....The shivers ran up and down my back, and I half expected to see those teamsters struck down by the hand of the Almighty....Each teamster had his own particular variety of oaths, each mule had a feminine name, and this brought the swearing down to a sort of personal basis."

Afterwards Mrs. Summerhayes had become something of a convert. "By the time we had crossed the great Mogollon Mesa, I had become accustomed to those dreadful oaths, and learned to admire the skill, persistency, and endurance shown by those rough teamsters. I actually got so far as to believe what Jack (her husband) told me about the swearing being necessary, for I saw impossible feats performed by the combination."

Anyone who has ever spit tobacco juice on a mule's behind from the seat of a wagon could have told her so.

The Rim country's most suitable place name was inspired by a card game in 1875 between two old settlers, Marion Clark and Corydon E. Cooley. The pair decided they were living too close together and one should move. They agreed to settle the matter with a game of cards called Seven-Up. On the last hand, Cooley needed only a point to win. "If you can show low, you win," Clark said. Cooley drew the deuce of clubs.

"Show low it is," he replied, and Show Low it is today.

*Campfire Recipes*

## BAKED CHICKEN IN A HOLE

You won't need a stove at all with this recipe.

Dig a hole about a foot square and two feet deep; fill it with firewood such as mesquite, oak, or juniper. (Charcoal briquets will work, too). Let the fire burn down to coals while you prepare a whole chicken. Use bread stuffing or just add a half-cup of water to the body cavity. Butter inside and out, and wrap with five or six layers of heavy-duty foil.

When the fire is ready, dig out half the coals, place the wrapped chicken (breast side up) in the hole, then cover with the remaining coals. Cover over with dirt so the heat can't escape. Allow three hours to cook the chicken. You'll be surprised how moist and flavorful it will be!

## CAMP DUNKIN' MATERIAL

Use the refrigerated biscuits that come in tubes to make quick and easy camp donuts. Poke a hole in the biscuit round, drop in hot fat to cook, then shake in a bag of cinnamon sugar or dredge in powdered sugar. Serve hot and be prepared to cook a bunch!

## TAKE A YOGURT BREAK

Going fishing or taking a short hike from camp? Take along a carton of frozen yogurt. By mid-morning, when a snack attack occurs, the yogurt will be thawed but still cold and tasty.

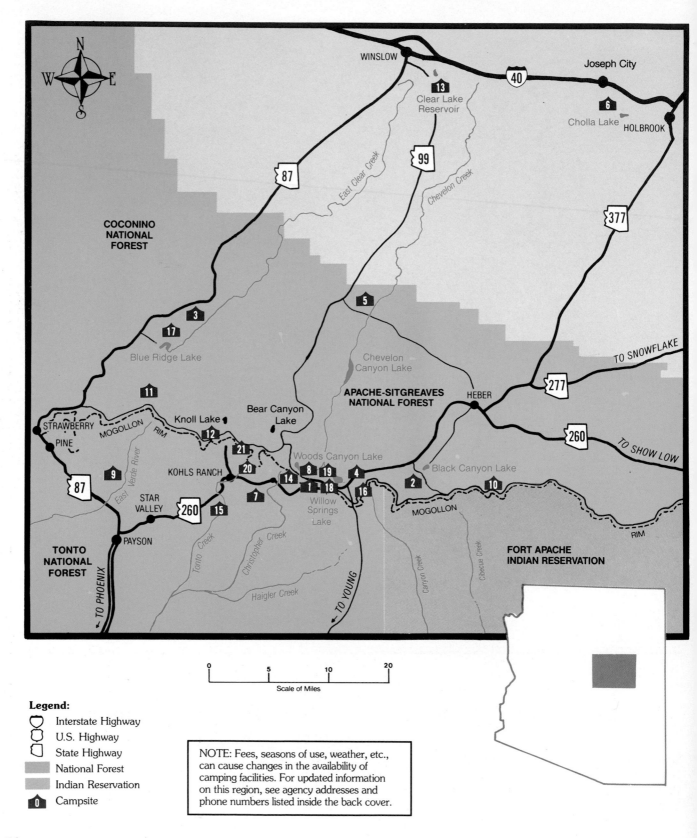

## Legend:
- **Interstate Highway**
- **U.S. Highway**
- **State Highway**
- National Forest
- Indian Reservation
- **Campsite**

NOTE: Fees, seasons of use, weather, etc., can cause changes in the availability of camping facilities. For updated information on this region, see agency addresses and phone numbers listed inside the back cover.

# Mogollon Rim Country Campsites

**Ponderosa** campground is just off State Route 260, about 15 miles east of Payson. There are 61 sites here, laid out in loops in a thick grove of pines. All interior roads are paved. Some sites provide pull-through access, some have back-in parking, and the rest are simply pullouts along the main road. Sites have table-bench units, standup grills, and fire rings. There are several water faucets and restrooms throughout the camp. The season here usually begins in early May and lasts until early October. A campground host is on hand to answer questions and help you find a site. Nearby is a pleasant self-guiding nature trail with small metal plaques to identify trees and shrubs.

**Tonto Creek** campground is on the banks of Tonto Creek, just across the road from Kohls Ranch and about 17 miles northeast of Payson on State Route 260. The 17 sites include some table-bench units with hand-laid stone pedestals, evidence of the age of this campground. Travel trailers longer than 16 feet are not permitted. Restrooms; water; fee; 7-day stay limit. Season is year-round.

**Upper Tonto Creek** is reached by driving up the access road alongside the creek, then turning right just before the first bridge. Ten sites in the tall pines; table-bench units, restrooms, and water. Stay limit is 7 days. Season is May to September. There are a couple of hiking-trail junctions right in the campground.

**Christopher Creek** campground is divided by the creek. The older sites are on the near side of the stream; a larger group has been laid out in a loop for those who ford the creek across a concrete apron. The main campground entrance is on the south side of State Route 260, about 22 miles east of Payson. The trees are mostly pines, with some oaks and junipers. User fee; stay limit, 7 days. Campground is open from May through September. It is very popular, so finding a spot on summer weekends isn't easy. Come early.

**Spillway** is one of two campgrounds at Woods Canyon. It can be reached by turning left for 4 miles on Forest Road 300 after State Route 260 tops out on the Rim. Spillway is on the lake shore and has 30 sites. Restrooms; water supply; the usual table-bench-grill units; waste disposal station within a half mile. Trailers 16 feet and under are permitted. Fee; stay limit, 14 days. This campground and nearby Aspen are among the most popular summer spots in the state; most sites are filled every day of summer. Season lasts from May to September.

Four new Rim country campgrounds have been opened by Apache-Sitgreaves: **Sink Hole, Rim, Crook,** and **Mogollon**. Designed alike, each has 34 units, a 14-day stay limit, a May through September season, restrooms, and a fee. They share the same safe-water station within a short drive of each. Sink Hole is on Forest Road 149 off State Route 260 as it tops out on the Rim. Boating and fishing are less than a mile away at Willow Springs Lake. Rim is 1 mile down Forest Road 300 off State Route 260, Crook is 3 miles farther and Mogollon is right next door.

| | RECREATION SITE NAME | APPROX. ELEV. | SEASONS OF USE | DAYS-LIMITS | FEE | NO. OF UNITS | SAFE WATER | 16 FT. RV LIMIT | WASTE DISP. | BOATING | FISHING |
|---|---|---|---|---|---|---|---|---|---|---|---|
| 1 | ASPEN | 7500 | May Sep. | 14 | X | 70 | X | | | X | X |
| 2 | BLACK CANYON RIM | 7600 | May Sep. | 14 | | 10 | | X | | | |
| 3 | BLUE RIDGE | 7300 | May Sep. | 14 | X | 10 | X | | | | |
| 4 | CANYON POINT | 7600 | May Sep. | 14 | X | 72 | X | | X | | |
| 5 | CHEVELON CROSSING | 6300 | Mar. Dec. | 14 | | 7 | | | | | X |
| 6 | CHOLLA LAKE | 5100 | All Yr. | 14 | X | 15 | X | | | X | X |
| 7 | CHRISTOPHER CREEK | 5600 | May Sep. | 7 | X | 43 | X | | | | X |
| 8 | CROOK | 7500 | May Sep. | 14 | X | 34 | X | | X | X | X |
| 9 | EAST VERDE REC. AREA | 5000 | May Sep. | 14 | | | | | | | X |
| 10 | GENTRY | 7700 | May Sep. | 14 | | 6 | | X | | | |
| 11 | KEHL SPRINGS | 7500 | May Sep. | 14 | | 8 | | | | | |
| 12 | KNOLL LAKE | 7500 | May Sep. | 14 | X | 42 | X | | | X | X |
| 13 | McHOOD PARK | 4900 | All Yr. | 14 | X | 11 | X | | | | |
| 14 | MOGOLLON | 7500 | May Sep. | 14 | X | 34 | X | | | | |
| 15 | PONDEROSA | 5600 | May Oct. | 7 | X | 61 | X | | X | | |
| 16 | RIM | 7500 | May Sep. | 14 | X | 34 | | | | | |
| 17 | ROCK CROSSING | 7500 | May Sep. | 14 | X | 38 | X | | | X | X |
| 18 | SINK HOLE | 7500 | May Sep. | 14 | X | 34 | X | | | X | X |
| 19 | SPILLWAY | 7500 | May Sep. | 14 | X | 30 | X | X | | X | X |
| 20 | TONTO CREEK | 5600 | All Yr. | 7 | X | 17 | X | X | | | X |
| 21 | UPPER TONTO CREEK | 5600 | May Sep. | 7 | X | 10 | X | X | | | X |

# Campsites

**Aspen** has 70 sites on a hill overlooking the lake. Water; restrooms; table-bench units. Cool temperatures, spectacular views from the Rim, and the opportunity to rent a boat and do some rowing combine to give Aspen special appeal. Fee; 14-day stay limit; May-September season; waste disposal station within a half-mile. Grocery store at the lake.

**Chevelon Crossing** is a bit off the beaten track and is seldom crowded. It can be reached by turning northwest off Route 260 a mile or so west of Heber onto Forest Road 504. Chevelon Crossing is about 15 miles via an unpaved road that is passable for any sort of vehicle in dry weather but can get very sticky when wet or snow-covered. The road crosses Chevelon Creek on a bridge just before the campground.

There's also access from Winslow, via Forest Roads 34 and 504 and from Chevelon Lake on Forest Road 169. There are just 7 sites, a restroom, no water and thus no fee; a March to December season; and a 14-day stay limit. There are table-bench units, but campers must pack out their trash and garbage because there are no pick ups.

**Canyon Point** is the best campground on the Rim. It has 72 sites in a mix of pull-through, back-in, and pullout locations. Some have table-bench units and fire rings. Restrooms and water are available, and there's a dump station. Canyon Point customarily opens for Memorial Day weekend and closes after Labor Day. Fee; 14-day stay limit. Very popular, so plan to arrive early.

**Gentry** campground is on the Rim Road at the base of Gentry fire-lookout tower. Take the Black Canyon Lake turnoff from State Route 260 and stay on Forest Road 300. It's about 5 unpaved miles to the tower, which is right beside the road. Gentry is best for tenters. There are just 6 sites, with table-bench units and a restroom. No water; no fee. If a lookout is on duty in the tower, you may be invited to come up and enjoy the view.

**Black Canyon Rim** is at the junction of the Rim Road and the access road to Black Canyon Lake, about 2 miles off State Route 260 between Woods Canyon Lake and Heber. The lake is about 3 miles away. A restroom and a few table-bench units are provided, but this is primarily suitable for recreational vehicles or trailers. No fee.

**Knoll Lake** has 42 sites in a loop on a hill above the lake. Water faucet near the entrance; restrooms; table-bench units. Parking is in pullouts beside the road; tenters will be the only ones immediately adjacent to tables. Fee; stay limit, 14 days; May-September season. A walk across the road from the campground offers a good view of the rocky, pine-covered island that gives the lake its name.

**East Verde Recreation Area** is a collection of several undeveloped campgrounds popular in the summer for day and weekend use. The sites stretch along the banks of the East Verde River from 4 miles north of Payson on State Route 87 to 12 miles north (2

*(Left) The old cavalry road from Fort Apache to Camp Verde—now called General Crook's Trail—runs along the top of the Rim. Jerry Sieve*
*(Right) Hundred-mile views south from the Rim. Dick Dietrich*

more miles on Route 87 and 10 miles on Forest Road 199). No fee; 14-day stay limit; outhouses. Elevation ranges from 4600 feet to 5200 feet. Season is May-September. Trout fishing is a big draw.

**Kehl Springs** is small but gorgeous. Just 8 sites are tucked along one edge of a meadow and surrounded by an old log fence. Restrooms and table-bench units, but no drinking water and no fee. Season is May to September; stay limit, 14 days. Kehl Springs is about 5 miles east of State Route 87 on Forest Road 300 — the Rim Road. It's just a short hike south from the campground to the Rim's very edge and spectacular views of the Pine-Payson country. Elevation is 7500 feet.

From **Rock Crossing** it's easy to see how Blue Ridge Lake got its name. The ridges that march away to the east from this 38-site campground really do look blue at dusk. Breathtaking views are offered from some of the sites along the eastern edge of the loop, and the ridge falls away sharply just a few yards from the table-bench area. Fee; water; restrooms; good access to all sites. Season is May-September. Blue Ridge Lake is about 3 miles east. State Route 87 is 3 miles west by unpaved but good road.

**Blue Ridge** campground comprises 10 units in the pines and oaks of the Coconino National Forest. Ac-cess is off State Route 87, about 8 miles north of the Clints Well junction, then a mile south on Forest Road 138. Fee; 14-day stay limit. Water; restroom; table-bench units. Open from May to September.

**McHood Park** is perched next to the canyon that holds Clear Creek. A small lake is backed up at this spot 6 miles south of Winslow on State Route 99. There are 11 campsites, 3 with water and electricity hookups. A restroom building with showers serves campers and the picnickers that make the park popular in the spring and summer. A new dock and paved boat-launch ramp are adjacent to the campground. Open all year; fee. McHood is administered by the City of Winslow.

**Cholla Lake** is a bonus for campers, fishermen and hunters. The lake, 1 mile east of Joseph City on Interstate 40, was created by the construction of the Cholla power plant; the water used in the plant's operation is stored in a huge 360-acre cooling pond. There are 15 campsites here, some with water and electricity hookups, a boat dock and launch ramp, and a swimming beach. The campground is open all year and since the lake's waters are warm, they never freeze. That makes fishing possible year-round. This is a Navajo County park. Fee; 14-day stay limit.

# The White Mountains

The White Mountains are both a specific place and a state of mind. There is a range in eastern Arizona called the White Mountains—forested giants that reach more than 11,000 feet high and collect rain and snow that supply much of the water for desert communities far down the White, Black, and Salt rivers. There's also a general area identified by the same name and defined a bit differently by each visitor, according to his memories. When someone says "White Mountains," perhaps the Pinetop sign blinks on in the brain; or you hear the soft complaint of tent pegs being driven somewhere in the campground, or you catch the fresh scent of spruce and fir behind an afternoon shower.

If there is a "most popular" Arizona camping region, this is it. The high, green, cool country of the White Mountains is a startling contrast to the state's arid lowlands, a surprise to newcomers, a treasured hideaway for long-time tent and recreational vehicle fans. Though more and more people—including campers —are discovering the delights of winter in the White Mountains, this is primarily a spring, summer, and fall destination, a celebration of three distinct seasons where nature seems to outdo herself.

Campground elevations vary from 6000 feet at Lyman Lake to more than 9000 at Hannagan Meadow, so it's difficult to pinpoint the beginning of the spring camping season. Lyman seldom freezes, and the first-class state park campground there is open year-round, so the vanguard of spring campers often alights at places like Lyman or the Navajo County park at Show Low Lake as early as the beginning of April. Snow at higher elevations begins to disappear in April, and by early May the roads and the lakes are open.

Most of the campgrounds in the White Mountains —except for those on the Fort Apache Indian Reservation (see pages 66 through 79)—are administered by the Apache-Sitgreaves National Forest. With a few exceptions, the Forest Service facilities open late in May and close after the Labor Day weekend.

Fall, especially, is a delightful time in these mountains. The annual color show begins in late September, atop the highest peaks, then as October wears on, aspen, oak, maple, locust, sumac, and all the other performers in the autumn parade take their places on stage. Remember those magic days called Indian summer, when the air is crisp and clean and nights are just right for good sleeping? That is October at Greer and Big Lake and Greens Peak. The crowds are gone, all is serene, and even restless nature seems to pause and relax between the powerful storms of summer and the rigors of the icy winter ahead.

For campers, there are more choices here than in any other part of Arizona. You can make your temporary home in one of the large, modern campgrounds like Big Lake or Hoyer or Winn or quietly escape to an almost unknown retreat such as South Fork or KP Cienega.

This happy state of affairs makes for difficult decisions, and some families set about collecting weekends at different campgrounds the way other people fill albums with stamps or display-case shelves with ceramic owls.

Add the opportunity to camp outside developed areas—permitted in the Apache-Sitgreaves—and there is literally a different White Mountain camping spot waiting for every weekend for the rest of your life. Except for a few places around heavily used recreation areas like Big Lake and Greer (which are posted), you can pretty well choose any side road in the national forest, leave civilization a few hundred yards behind, and set up camp in some silent clearing among the firs and aspens. Leave it as pristine as you found it, and we can continue to enjoy this privilege.

If you're heading for the high country for the first time, it's sometimes hard to imagine just how cool it will be. When it's a hundred-degree July day in Phoenix or Tucson, and you're packing for a week at, say, Luna Lake, you tend not to think about sweaters, jackets, gloves, and stocking caps. You'll be in shorts and T-shirts during the sunny days, of course; but those sweaters and jackets will come in handy early and late in the day, or during sudden showers that may well include a little hail. Even in midsummer, nighttime temperatures can dip to the 30s.

Summer approaches and so do thoughts of the White Mountains: a campsite with walls of thick-growing spruce, rain drumming on canvas or aluminum, cold wine and warm campfires, old friends and new memories.

*(Right) The view from Escudilla Mountain, one of the tallest of the White Mountain peaks. The peaks hold snow eight or nine months of the year, giving the range its name.* Jerry Jacka

54

(Above) A campsite near Hannagan Meadow, along U.S. Route 666, south of Alpine. Don B. Stevenson
(Right) The highest quality of all "quality time"—trying for a stringer of rainbows for lunch. Ernie Weegen
(Below) Cooking up a mess of fresh trout. Christine Keith

(Above) Why they post those signs that say "Deer Crossing." James Tallon
(Below) Set up for a stay along the East Fork of the Black River. Jerry Sieve
(Left) Campers enjoy the beauty of meadows full of summer wildflowers. David Muench

# The Legend of Red Ghost

Most folks will tell you camels are not found in Arizona's high country. Truth is, those adaptable beasts can thrive in just about any kind of terrain. The U. S. Army introduced camels to the Southwest back in the 1850s, using them as beasts of burden while surveying a road across northern Arizona. But the Civil War interrupted the great camel experiment, and most of the homely critters were sold at auction. A few were turned loose to run wild—and therein lies the basis for the legend of Red Ghost.

The story begins back in 1883 at a lonely ranch near Eagle Creek in southeastern Arizona. The Apache wars were drawing to a close; however, a few renegade bands were on the prowl, keeping isolated ranches in a constant state of siege. Early one morning two men rode out to check on the livestock, leaving their wives at the ranch with the children. About midmorning, one of the women went down to the spring to fetch a bucket of water while the other remained in the house with the children.

Suddenly one of the dogs began to bark ferociously. The woman inside the house heard a terrifying scream. Looking out the window, she saw a huge, reddish-hued beast run by with a devilish-looking creature on its back.

The frightened woman barricaded herself in the house and waited anxiously for the men to return. That night they found the body of the other woman, trampled to death. Next day tracks were found, cloven hoof prints much larger than those of a horse, along with long strands of reddish hair.

A few days later a party of prospectors near Clifton were awakened by the sound of thundering hoofs and ear-piercing screams. Their tent collapsed, and the men clawed their way out of the tangle just in time to see a gigantic creature run off in the moonlight. The next day they, too, found huge cloven-hoof prints and long, red strands of hair clinging to the brush.

Naturally these stories grew and were embellished by local raconteurs. One man claimed he saw the beast kill and eat a grizzly bear. Another insisted he had chased the Red Ghost, only to have it disappear before his eyes.

A few months after the incident with the miners, Cyrus Hamblin, a rancher on the Salt River, rode up on the animal while rounding up cows. Hamblin recognized the beast as a camel, with something tied to its back that resembled the skeleton of a man. Although Hamblin had a reputation as an honest man and one not given to tall tales, many refused to believe his story. Several weeks later, over on the Verde River, the camel was spotted again, this time by another group of prospectors. They, too, saw something attached to the animal's back. Grabbing their weapons they fired at the camel but missed. The animal bolted and ran, causing a piece of the strange object to fall to the ground. What the miners saw made the hair bristle on their necks. On the ground lay a human skull with some parts of flesh and hair still attached.

A few days later the Red Ghost struck again; this time the victims were teamsters camped beside a lonely road. They said they were awakened in the middle of the night by a loud scream. According to the terrified drivers, a creature at least thirty feet tall knocked over two freight wagons and generally raised hell with the camp. The men ran for their lives and hid in the brush. Returning the next day, they found cloven-hoof prints and red strands of hair.

About a year later, a cowboy near Phoenix came upon the Red Ghost eating grass in a corral. Traditionally, cowboys have been unable to resist the temptation to rope anything that wears hair, and this fellow was no exception. Forming a loop in his rope, he tossed it over the camel's head. Suddenly the angry beast turned and charged. The cowboy's horse tried to dodge, but to no avail. Horse and rider went down, and as the camel galloped off in a cloud of dust, the astonished cowboy recognized the skeletal remains of a man lashed to its back.

During the next few years, stories of the Red Ghost grew to legendary proportions. The creature appeared for the last time nine years later in eastern Arizona. A rancher awoke one morning and saw the huge animal casually grazing in his garden. He drew a careful bead with is trusty Winchester and dropped the beast with one shot. An examination of the corpse convinced all that this was indeed the fabled Red Ghost. The animal's back was heavily scarred from rawhide strips that had been used to tie down the body of a man. Some of the leather strands had cut into the camel's flesh. But how the human body came to be attached to the back of the camel remains a cruel mystery.

**Campfire Recipes**

### SHISH KABOB TIME

An aim of most camp cooks is to find easy, one-dish meals that offer variety and plenty of protein. Shish kabob—meat and vegetables on a skewer—does exactly that. You can prepare the meal ahead of time at home, wrap in foil, and keep in the ice chest. Or assemble the ingredients in plastic bags or wrap in individual foil packets; then let the campers combine their own. Cube (about 1 1/2 inches in size) inexpensive cuts of beef, and sprinkle with tenderizer (or use your favorite marinade). This is a good way to serve venison or elk, too. Alternate chunks of the meat with vegetables and other ingredients on a skewer, lay it on the grill over hot coals, turn once, and eat when done. Have a chilled salad and some wine or buttermilk ready, and you have a meal fit for the finest campground setting. Try any or all of these ingredients, cut to the right size: tomato; pineapple; mushroom; bacon; chili pepper; green bell pepper; onion; ripe olive; small, cooked new potato.

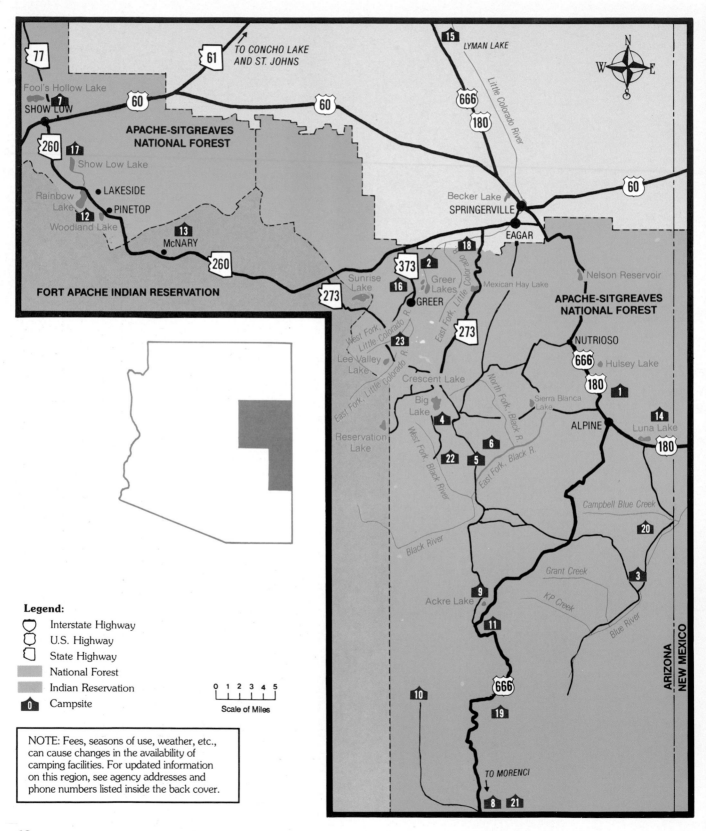

**Legend:**
- Interstate Highway
- U.S. Highway
- State Highway
- National Forest
- Indian Reservation
- 0 Campsite

0 1 2 3 4 5
Scale of Miles

NOTE: Fees, seasons of use, weather, etc., can cause changes in the availability of camping facilities. For updated information on this region, see agency addresses and phone numbers listed inside the back cover.

# White Mountain Campsites

**Rolfe C. Hoyer** campground, at 8500 feet, is a modern, 100-site showcase. The interior roads are paved, restrooms have running water and flush toilets, and there are pull-through and back-in sites for trailers and large recreational vehicles. There's also a sanitary disposal station.

Hoyer is set in the tall pines, about a mile north of the mountain community of Greer, and the access road to the 3 Greer lakes is just across from the campground entrance. The season is May to October. Starting date is adjusted to weather conditions, but the campground is always open by Memorial Day weekend. Check with the campground host for days and times of naturalist programs by forest rangers. There is a daily user fee. Stay limit is 14 days.

**Benny Creek**, named for Benny Howell, is about a mile north of Hoyer. In 1897, Benny thought he was all set to marry Rosey Thompson (another creek named after her is just north of here); but when he rode into town to get the license, she ran off and married Fred Hoffman. So, like their namesakes, Benny and Rosey creeks run close together but never join. (How's that for a little romance with your campground information?)

Benny Creek has 30 sites in a thick grove of pines. Table-bench units; grills; restrooms. Safe water. Fee; 14-day stay limit; May-October season. An easy, very pleasant drive from Pinetop or Springerville.

**Winn** campground, like others of the newer Forest Service camps, is built well away from a main road. It is about a mile off State Route 273 as that road winds from Sunrise Lake toward Big Lake. The Winn turnoff is opposite the road to Lee Valley Lake, about 7 miles south of Sunrise.

There are 63 sites here, laid out in loops in the pine-spruce-fir forest. At 9300 feet, Winn is the highest campground in the national forest — the closest to heaven. Pull-through sites, table-bench units, and water faucets, as well as restrooms, are scattered through the campground. User fee; 14-day stay limit. Season runs from Memorial Day weekend to October. Anglers staying at Winn can walk a few hundred yards north, drop into the canyon that holds the West Fork of the Little Colorado, and in 20 minutes be fishing for rainbow trout downstream from Sheep Crossing.

**Big Lake** is one of the most popular camping and fishing spots in the White Mountains. The main campground, called **Rainbow**, has 160 sites, water, and modern restrooms. The beautifully selected sites occupy a thickly wooded ridge above the lake. Check with the visitor center for the schedule of nature walks and naturalist programs. Fee; 14-day stay limit;

| RECREATION SITE NAME | APPROX. ELEV. | SEASONS OF USE | DAYS-LIMITS | FEE | NO. OF UNITS | SAFE WATER | 16 FT. RV LIMIT | WASTE DISP. | BOATING | FISHING |
|---|---|---|---|---|---|---|---|---|---|---|
| 1 ALPINE DIVIDE | 8500 | May Sep. | 14 | X | 10 | X | | | | |
| 2 BENNY CREEK | 8500 | May Oct. | 14 | X | 30 | X | | | | X |
| 3 BLUE CROSSING | 6200 | May Oct. | 14 | | 4 | | | | | X |
| 4A BIG LAKE BROOK CHAR | 9000 | May Sep. | 14 | X | 55 | | | | X | X |
| 4B CUTTHROAT | 9000 | May Sep. | 14 | X | | | | | X | X |
| 4C GRAYLING | 9000 | May Sep. | 14 | X | | | | | X | X |
| 4D RAINBOW | 9000 | May Sep. | 14 | X | 160 | X | | X | X | X |
| 5 BUFFALO CROSSING | 7600 | May Oct. | 14 | | 20 | | | | | X |
| 6 DIAMOND ROCK | 7900 | May Oct. | 14 | | 12 | X | | | | X |
| 7 FOOL'S HOLLOW | 6600 | May Oct. | 14 | | 20 | | | | X | X |
| 8 GRANVILLE | 6600 | May Sep. | 14 | | 9 | X | | X | | |
| 9 HANNAGAN | 9100 | May Sep. | 14 | | 8 | | | | | |
| 10 HONEYMOON | 5400 | May Sep. | 14 | | 4 | | X | | | |
| 11 K.P. CIENEGA | 9000 | May Sep. | 14 | | 5 | X | | | | |
| 12 LAKESIDE | 7000 | May Sep. | 14 | X | 83 | X | | | X | X |
| 13 LOS BURROS | 8000 | May Sep. | 14 | | 20 | | | | | |
| 14 LUNA LAKE | 8000 | May Sep. | 14 | X | 50 | X | | | X | X |
| 15 LYMAN LAKE | 6000 | All Yr. | 14 | X | 67 | X | | X | X | X |
| 16 ROLFE C. HOYER | 8500 | May Oct. | 14 | X | 100 | X | | X | X | X |
| 17 SHOW LOW LAKE | 7000 | Apr. Nov. | 14 | X | 75 | X | | | X | X |
| 18 SOUTH FORK | 7700 | May Nov. | 14 | | 8 | | | | | X |
| 19 STRAYHORSE | 7800 | May Sep. | 14 | | 6 | X | | | | |
| 20 UPPER BLUE | 6200 | May Oct. | 14 | | 3 | | | | | X |
| 21 Upper & Lower JUAN MILLER | 6000 | May Sep. | 14 | | 8 | | X | | | |
| 22 WEST FORK | 7600 | May Oct. | 14 | | 20 | | | | | X |
| 23 WINN | 9300 | May Oct. | 14 | X | 63 | X | | | X | X |

# Campsites

sanitary disposal station. Season extends from Memorial Day weekend to Labor Day.

Three other Big Lake campgrounds, **Grayling, Brook Char,** and **Cutthroat**, are near the store and boat dock on the lakeshore. Together they provide 55 sites. Grayling is open as long as the road to the lake permits access. The sites at Brook Char and Cutthroat are on the hill just behind the store and overlook the boat launch ramp. All are subject to the 14-day stay limit, and all have user fees.

The store sells groceries, gasoline, propane, ice, and fishing supplies. It's also a source of rental boats and lots of good, free fishing advice.

**Buffalo Crossing** is 10 miles south of Big Lake on Forest Road 24. There are 20 sites here, sprinkled along the East Fork of the Black River. The area is a big favorite with the recreational vehicle owners, since there is plenty of room for trailers and motor homes. No drinking water; no user fee; 14-day stay limit. The stream is stocked weekly with rainbow trout from early May to Labor Day. The campground is open from early May through October.

**Diamond Rock** is just upstream from Buffalo Crossing, on the East Fork of the Black River. Twelve sites are available with table-bench units, restrooms, and a central water supply. No fee; 14-day stay limit. The season is the same as at Buffalo Crossing. There are neither buffalo nor diamonds here, but good camping with lots of fishing opportunities.

**West Fork** campground is about 6 miles west and north of Buffalo Crossing on the West Fork of the Black River. Twenty sites are scattered along the stream, with plenty of room for recreational vehicles. Table-bench units and restrooms are available, but no water. No fee; 14-day stay limit. Season is early May to October. The creek is stocked regularly with rainbow trout throughout the summer. You'll also find stream-hatched brown trout both upstream and downstream. An alternate access route is Forest Road 68, south of Big Lake down Conklin Ridge. Early and late in the day, this route is a good one for sighting deer and turkey. The entire area is rich in autumn color in early October.

**Alpine Divide** campground, bordering U. S. Route 666 about 4 miles north of Alpine, is in the forest at the foot of a steep hill. Easy access to most sites; drinking water and restrooms at all 10 of them. User fee; 14-day stay limit. Season is early May through September.

**Luna Lake** campground is in a parklike setting in the pines north of the lake and away from the highway. Luna is about 4 miles from the tiny community of Alpine, which offers all services. Fifty sites, a campground host; water and restrooms; and a steady supply of trout from the lake. Fee; 14-day stay limit. A May to September season, which may change a bit depending on the weather. There's a small store at the lake, with fishing tackle for sale and boats for rent. The lake has a good launch ramp, and motors up to 8 horsepower are permitted.

**Hannagan** campground is named for Robert Hannagan, a New Mexico cattleman who brought his herds to the meadows in this area in the mid-1880s. Eight sites; restrooms; no water; no fee; 14-day stay limit. The campground is open from May through September. Hannagan is 23 miles south of Alpine on U.S. Route 666, and the drive offers one of the most spectacular fall-color tours in the state—including extensive yellow-gold displays of colorful aspens.

**K P Cienega** (Cienega means marsh) is a 5-site campground on the edge of a spectacular meadow. The elevation here is 9000 feet. The campground, a short distance off U.S. Route 666 about 29 miles south of Alpine, is a small loop in the edge of the spruce-fir-aspen forest. Restroom; no fee. The log fence around the camp and the nearby corral indicate the age of the facility. K P Cienega is still popular with horsemen on trail rides. Count yourself lucky if you find a space here anytime from May to September.

**Blue Crossing** is a 4-unit campground at the bottom of Forest Road 567. The road winds from U.S. Route 666 down the spine of a long, steep ridge to the Blue River and an unbridged crossing. No drinking water; no fee; 14-day stay limit. Elevation is 6200 feet; the season is May to October. It's lonesome, awesome country.

**Upper Blue** is another small campground on the Blue River, with 3 sites, a 14-day stay limit, and a May-October season. No fee. Upper Blue campground is 6 miles upriver from Blue Crossing—or you can take Forest Road 281 from Alpine.

**Strayhorse** is just off U. S. Route 666 about 32 miles south of Alpine. This 6-unit campground is at 7800 feet, after the point where you take the plunge off the Mogollon Rim toward Clifton. Water; no fee; 14-day stay limit; a May-September season.

**Honeymoon** campground could be, in fact, a good place for a honeymoon. It's about 50 miles north and west of Clifton, under the Rim on Eagle Creek. No trailers over 16 feet, because of the narrow, twisting access road. Four units; no water; no fee; a May-September season. You have to want to camp here, because it's really off the beaten track.

**Upper** and **Lower Juan Miller** are at the 6000-foot level along U.S. Route 666, about 27 miles north of Clifton. Together the campgrounds have 8 sites. No water; no fee. Just beautiful views of the rugged countryside.

**Granville** campground has 9 units. It's located along U.S. Route 666 about 16 miles north of Clifton at an elevation of 6600 feet. Water; no fee. The season is May-September. This is the area of the fabled Coronado Trail. Before you drift off to sleep, imagine Coronado and his men struggling through this up-and-down country more than 450 years ago, in search of the nonexistent Seven Cities of Gold.

**South Fork** is a small but charming campground on the banks of the South Fork of the Little Colorado. Eight sites are scattered through the pines, and hand-built log bridges span the small stream. No drinking water; no fee; 14-day stay limit; a May-November season. Access is from State Route 260 about 5 miles west of Eagar.

**Los Burros,** 7 miles north of McNary off State Route 260 on Forest Road 224, is a 20-unit campground. High in the Apache-Sitgreaves National Forest at 8,000 feet, the site has a May through September season, a 14-day stay limit, restrooms, and no fee.

**Lakeside** campground is beside State Route 260 in the lively community of Lakeside. This 83-unit camp is only a block from Rainbow Lake. It has restrooms, water at various places, and some pull-through sites. Elevation is 7000 feet. Campground is open from about May-September, depending on the weather. All services within walking distance. Fee; 14-day stay limit.

**Fool's Hollow** is within the city limits of Show Low off Old Linden Road and 32nd Avenue. Fool's Hollow has 20 sites and no fee. Restrooms are its only amenity. Two-week stay limit; elevation of 6600 feet; May through October season. Small boats can bring anglers closer to their catch.

**Show Low Lake** is a Navajo County park. Its 75 campsites are situated on the hill overlooking the lake. There are table-bench units, restrooms, and a water supply. User fee; season usually April to November. Paved access is off State Route 260 about 5 miles southeast of Show Low. (A hospital is nearby, in case of emergency.) Good trout fishing, a small store, boat rentals.

**Lyman Lake** is part of the state park system. The campground location is excellent, on the hill overlooking the lake and swimming beach. There are ramadas, hot showers, a sanitary disposal station, and a total of 67 sites. At 6000 feet, temperatures are moderate, and the campground is open year-round. The sites include 25 with water and electric hookups. Boat-launch ramp. Access is via a 1-mile paved road from U.S. Route 666 about 11 miles south of St. Johns. Bonus: A small herd of buffalo grazes beside the access road, where it leaves U. S. 666. The youngsters can get a close-up view of the shaggy beasts. Special programs are conducted upon request.

*Winn campground, a popular stopping place in the high country near Lee Valley Lake. Jerry Sieve*

# The Fort Apache Reservation

The homeland of the White Mountain Apache Tribe—the Fort Apache Indian Reservation—is more than 1.5 million acres of mountainous terrain in east-central Arizona, mostly timbered and mostly well watered. Its streams and rivers, along with man-made lakes built for fishing and recreation, make it a very popular destination for Arizona campers.

Because the Indians have jurisdiction here, there are special fees, rules, and regulations. And though the old ways still have great influence in Apache culture, tribal members are part of the modern world. Pickup trucks, color television, blue jeans, the Colonel's fried chicken work their universal appeal. Still, many newcomers to the state are uneasy about visiting the Indian reservations, not sure of their welcome, slightly inhibited by the rugged surroundings and the unfamiliar people.

The Apache understand this feeling, and, since the late 1950s, they have made a special effort to make visitors welcome. Far from merely tolerating those who want to enjoy the Apache country's outdoor recreation opportunities, the Indians have actively promoted reservation camping, hunting, fishing, and winter sports. So you are encouraged to take advantage of Apache facilities and Apache friendship.

Camping is possible all year, but most visitors either come when the fishing gets good in the early spring or wait until summer to enjoy the 7000- to 9000-foot elevations. The same heights that guarantee abundant pine, spruce, aspen, and fir can also permit nighttime temperatures to drop below freezing early and late in the April-to-November span. Even in July and August, frost can form on the meadow grasses at the higher campgrounds, although daytime highs may be in the 80s.

Summer showers begin in early July, and there are short, spectacular downpours almost every afternoon during July, August, and the first part of September. The day begins clear and cool, but as the air heats up, fluffy white cumulus clouds form over the peaks of Baldy and Ord—and sometime after noon the rain sweeps down, freshening the air and dampening the dust on the back roads.

Some of those back roads get a bit bumpy and/or muddy after awhile. But better roads and better road signing are part of the Apache's ongoing campaign to attract more outdoorsmen, and generally all the campgrounds are accessible by any sort of recreational vehicle.

Part of the charm of Apache country is the chance to choose a remote campground and thus escape the crowds. That takes some planning and initiative and may represent a nod to the past, when camping depended more on individual ingenuity and resourcefulness and less on parking a fully equipped recreational vehicle on a compact piece of pavement. Still, whatever your camping mode, the Apache welcome you to one of the state's most beautiful areas.

Campgrounds on the Fort Apache reservation are all located close to water—lakes or streams. There's usually plenty of room; Apache campgrounds are seldom full, even on holiday weekends. You'll find the campgrounds pleasantly unstructured, different from the highly organized, paved, cheek-by-jowl sites offered at some of the new federal facilities elsewhere in the state. The layouts suggest that perhaps a group of friends came to the grove of trees along the lakeshore and each chose a spot that appealed to him; then, when everyone was settled, they called it a campground.

There are some large facilities, notably the 200-unit campground at Sunrise, on a densely forested ridge a short walk from the lake; Horseshoe Cienega Lake, where aspen trees shade the widely dispersed sites; and popular Hawley Lake, often the source of Arizona's lowest temperature as reported on television weathercasts. At the other end of the scale are the one- or two-family sites like those sprinkled along the banks of Diamond Creek. Add several dozen places that are not formally classified as campgrounds, offering only a place to park, a 55-gallon drum for garbage, a table-bench unit—and a huge helping of solitude.

The Apache charge campers daily fees, but they generally are no more than those assessed by the national forests that surround the reservation—and, in either case, the camper is getting a real bargain. For half the cost of a tank of gas, you can enjoy a long weekend at Drift Fence Lake, McCoy Bridge on the North Fork of the White River, or the charming campground at Reservation Lake.

*(Right) A camp along the North Fork of the White River, in the heart of the Apache high country, well timbered and well watered. Ernie Weegen*

(Top) *Firelight fascination.* Don B. Stevenson
(Above) *The first long swallow of cool, sweet water.*
Fred Griffin
(Left) *The broad sweep of the White Mountain Apache homeland, where campers are welcome year around.*
Jerry Jacka
(Following panel) *Hurricane Lake, one of the Apache impoundments built solely for recreation, is nestled at the foot of Mount Baldy at an elevation of 9000 feet.*
Dick Dietrich
(Inset) *A quiet camping spot at Reservation Lake.*
James Tallon

(Above) The huge ski complex developed by the Apaches at Sunrise has helped turn the White Mountains into a four-season playground. Don B. Stevenson
(Left) Lunchtime at one of Sunrise's lodges. Don B. Stevenson

(Below left) A class of beginners waits awkwardly for the first lesson; by tomorrow they'll graduate to the lower slopes. J. Peter Mortimer
(Right) Snow camping offers unique challenges and great satisfaction. The winter snow creates silence and peace not found at any other time of the year. Gill Kenney

# The Fabulous Lost Adams Diggings

## Around the Campfire

Somewhere out in these rugged mountains—just maybe—lies the greatest mystery mine of them all, the Lost Adams. According to legend, a sheer wall with a huge boulder at the base hides a narrow opening into a Z-shaped canyon, called by the Apaches *Sno-ta-hay.* This hidden canyon opens up into a small valley bisected by a stream. Beneath the floor of a burned-out cabin lie several buckskin sacks containing millions of dollars (at today's prices) in gold dust. For more than a century, treasure seekers have searched in vain for the entrance to that fabled canyon.

The story began along the Gila Trail in the mid-1860s. A freighter named Adams was camped near Gila Bend when a band of Apaches drove off his team of horses. Adams grabbed his rifle and ran off in pursuit. He eventually caught up with the animals, but upon returning to camp he found that his wagon had been ransacked and burned.

Adams rode to the Pima villages on the Gila River hoping to barter for supplies. He arrived there to find a party of some twenty miners, all excited over the prospect of getting rich. A young Mexican who had escaped from the Apache Indians had arrived with a tale of Apache gold. One of the youngster's ears had been twisted into a grotesque knot, a deformity that inspired the name "Gotch Ear". He'd been captured as a child and had grown up with the band, but then had a fight with one of the warriors and killed him. Fearing retaliation from the slain man's relatives, he fled. On his way to Sonora, Mexico, he met the American prospectors.

"I know a canyon where you might load a horse with gold in one day's gathering," he told them. "There are pieces as big as acorns, scattered on the ground. Above the gravel is a rock holding chunks of this yellow stuff as big as a wild turkey's egg."

The gold, the boy said, was located in a hidden canyon in the heart of Apacheria.

With promises of a couple of horses, a red bandanna, a rifle, and a hundred dollars, the argonauts persuaded "Gotch Ear" to lead them to the Apache treasure. Adams' timely arrival at the Pima villages provided the animals essential to the trek. The twenty prospectors were without horses, and none were to be found among the Pimas; so Adams was invited to join up. Since he had lost everything in the Apache raid, he now figured to recoup some of his losses.

Adams' account of the next few days' journey tells of traveling northeast from the Pima villages toward Mount Ord in the Mazatzals. From there the party headed across the rugged central mountains south of the Mogollon Rim. Finally they approached a steep cliff. When one of the miners wondered if they were going to scale the wall, "Gotch Ear" just smiled and said, "Wait and see." He led them around a large boulder at the foot of the wall and through a hidden puerto or door that led into a narrow, Z-shaped canyon.

A short distance farther, they came to a beautiful valley threaded by a stream. At the far end of this box canyon was a waterfall.

"If you search the gravel at the water's edge," the Mexican youth advised, "you'll find the yellow metal you seek."

Soon after, the canyon walls rocked with the sound of whooping and hollering as the prospectors filled their sacks with gold nuggets.

"Gotch Ear" was rewarded generously, and he rode off into the darkness, never to be seen again.

A few days later, Chief Nana and about thirty of his warriors paid a call. He told the prospectors they would be allowed to stay as long as they remained below the falls, but under no circumstances was anyone to travel any farther up the canyon.

Over the next few days, the miners set up camp. Some built a log cabin, a few hunted, while the rest panned the nugget-laden stream. The gold was loaded in buckskin bags and placed in a hole beneath the cabin's hearth. When supplies ran low, a small party was sent to Fort Wingate, New Mexico, to purchase more.

Despite the stern warning of the Apache chief, Nana, a few curious prospectors climbed above the falls searching for golden boulders "the size of wild turkeys' eggs." And they found some. One brought back a coffee pot half-filled with nuggets.

Meanwhile the supply party was a few days late returning, so Adams and a man named Davidson went to search for them. Near the hidden entrance to the canyon, circling buzzards provided the first mute warning of tragedy. Adams and Davidson quickly buried the bodies of the supply party in shallow graves and hurried back to camp to give warning. Long before they reached the little valley, they heard the war cries of the Apaches. The wary pair crept close enough to see the bloody massacre's aftermath before making their way back through the canyon.

Several days later, an army patrol from a camp near the future site of Fort Apache discovered Adams and Davidson, dazed and delirious from their torturous ordeal. The soldiers carried them into camp, where Davidson soon died. Adams recovered and went to California. All he had to show for his efforts was a solitary gold nugget—about the size of a wild turkey's egg.

Adams returned to Arizona after the Apache wars ended and spent the rest of his life trying to relocate the Z-shaped canyon called *Sno-ta-hay.* His long, unsuccessful quest ended with his death at the age of 93.

## Campfire Recipes

### MORE FOIL COOKING

Using foil, cook corn on the cob right along with the fish or other meat. Buy roasting ears that have not been stripped. Carefully peel back the husk, remove the "silk," and add a teaspoon of butter; then re-cover the ear with the husk and double-wrap in foil. Cook for fifteen to twenty minutes on the grill or in the coals, turning often to avoid burning, and you'll have the best corn you've ever eaten.

Pre-bake potatoes at home in the oven or microwave, double-wrap in foil, and finish cooking in camp—in the coals or on the grill. The potatoes will be uniformly done—no more "burned on the outside, raw on the inside."

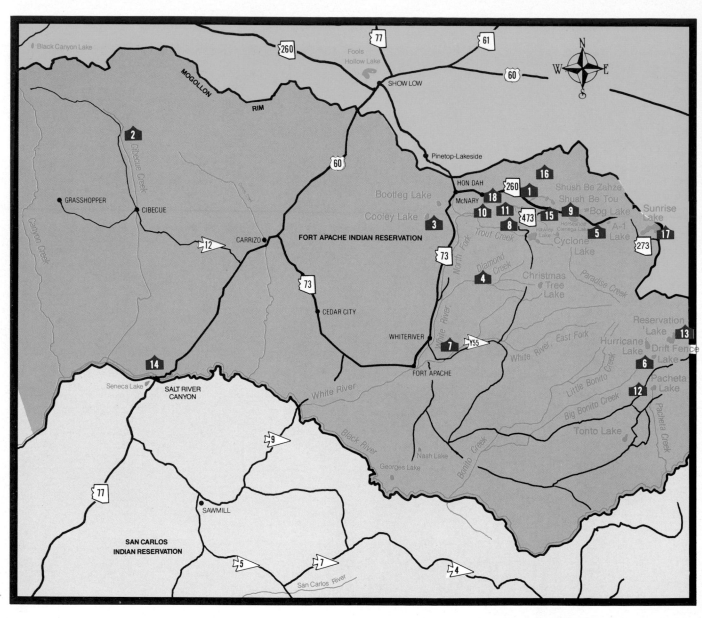

Black Canyon Lake

MOGOLLON RIM

260

77

Fools Hollow Lake

61

60

SHOW LOW

N
W E
S

2

Cibecue Creek

Deep Creek

GRASSHOPPER

CIBECUE

Canyon Creek

Pinetop-Lakeside

60

HON DAH

McNARY

Bootleg Lake

Cooley Lake

16

260

18

1

10

11

8

473

15

9

Shush Be Zahze

Shush Be Tou

Bog Lake

Sunrise Lake

Horseshoe Cienega Lake

Hawley Lake

5

A-1 Lake

17

273

12

CARRIZO

FORT APACHE INDIAN RESERVATION

3

73

73

CEDAR CITY

73

North Fork

Trout Creek

4

Diamond Creek

Cyclone Lake

Christmas Tree Lake

Paradise Creek

WHITERIVER

White River

7

55

White River, East Fork

Reservation Lake

13

Hurricane Lake

Drift Fence Lake

6

14

FORT APACHE

SALT RIVER CANYON

Seneca Lake

White River

Black River

9

Little Bonito Creek

Big Bonito Creek

Pacheta Lake

12

Tonto Lake

Pacheta Creek

Bonito Creek

Nash Lake

Georges Lake

77

SAWMILL

SAN CARLOS INDIAN RESERVATION

5

7

4

San Carlos River

0    5    10    15    20
Scale of Miles

**Legend:**

 Interstate Highway

U.S. Highway

State Highway

Reservation Route

National Forest

Indian Reservation

0 Campsite

NOTE: Fees, seasons of use, weather, etc., can cause changes in the availability of camping facilities. For updated information on this region, see agency addresses and phone numbers listed inside the back cover.

# Fort Apache Reservation Campsites

Unlike the national forests that surround it, the Fort Apache Indian Reservation is not open to camping except in specified, developed campgrounds. There are plenty of those, however, with more than a 1000 individual sites. All are water-oriented, from the biggest campground at Sunrise Lake to the 1- or 2-family sites scattered along Diamond Creek for more than 20 miles. The Apache facilities tend to be a bit more on the primitive side than Forest Service camps, not quite so strictly laid out and managed. Many campers appreciate this casualness. Tribal campgrounds are usually much less crowded than other high country areas, too. If you've been rebuffed by "full" signs at national forest campgrounds, the Apache sites look very good indeed. Snowfall November through April severely restricts access to the sites.

**Upper Log Road** has 95 sites scattered along the North Fork of the White River, above and below the bridged crossing where Trout Creek empties into the White. There are wood table-bench units, garbage barrels, and waterless restrooms (the so-called pit toilets). No drinking water is available here, but many of the sites are right along the river, and it is one of the most popular camping areas on the reservation.

**Lower Log Road** is about 3 or 4 miles downstream from the upper campground and has 40 sites distributed in the same way. The facilities are similar. Again, no drinking water. Both Log Road campgrounds are 6500 to 7000 feet in elevation, so night temperatures are milder than at most other reservation sites.

**Cooley Lake** has 6 places to park a camper or pitch a tent. It offers table-bench units and a restroom. No drinking water.

**Bog Creek** campground consists of only 5 sites, but they are on a slight slope above the creek and in a parklike stand of trees. Nothing fancy: minimum facilities, no drinking water. The camp sits beside State Route 260 east of McNary.

**Shush Be Zahze Lake** (Little Bear) is mostly do-it-yourself, with about 20 sites, some without tables, that are intended for self-contained campers. Located on a ridge overlooking the lake, it has minimum facilities. Drinking water is within a half-mile.

**Shush Be Tou Lake** (Big Bear) shares an access road with Little Bear. There is a dependable drinking water source on your right just after you turn off State Route 260. Sites are casual, as at Little Bear, and facilities are minimal.

**Horseshoe Cienega Lake** has 68 widely dispersed sites, and is one of the largest and best of the Apache campgrounds. It's on the south shore of the lake in a stand of mixed conifer and aspen trees. Table-bench units, restrooms, and boat launch ramp. Drinking water faucets, shut off October-May, are scattered through the campground. Horseshoe is just off State Route 260, about 10 miles east of McNary. A store and boat dock with rental boats are operated May-September.

**Hawley Lake** has paved access via State Route 473. A hundred campsites extend along the shore.

| RECREATION SITE NAME | APPROX. ELEV. | SEASONS OF USE | DAYS-LIMITS | FEE | NO. OF UNITS | SAFE WATER | 16 FT. RV LIMIT | WASTE DISP. | BOATING | FISHING |
|---|---|---|---|---|---|---|---|---|---|---|
| 1 BOG CREEK | 7500 | All Yr. | | X | 5 | | | | | X |
| 2 CIBECUE CREEK | 6500 | All Yr. | | X | 10 | | | | | X |
| 3 COOLEY LAKE | 7000 | All Yr. | | X | 6 | | | | X | X |
| 4 DIAMOND CREEK | 8300 | May Nov. | | X | 25 | | | | | X |
| 5 DITCH CAMP | 8300 | All Yr. | | X | 35 | | | | | X |
| 6 DRIFT FENCE LAKE | 8000 | May Nov. | | X | 20 | | | | X | X |
| 7 EAST FORK | 6000 | May Nov. | | X | 12 | | | | | X |
| 8 HAWLEY LAKE | 8500 | All Yr. | | X | 100 | X | | | X | X |
| 9 HORSESHOE CIENEGA LAKE | 8500 | All Yr. | | X | 68 | X | | X | X | X |
| 10 LOWER LOG ROAD | 6500 | All Yr. | | X | 40 | | | | | X |
| 11 McCOY BRIDGE | 7500 | All Yr. | | X | | | | | | X |
| 12 PACHETA LAKE | 8500 | May Nov. | | X | 25 | | | | X | X |
| 13 RESERVATION LAKE | 9500 | May Nov. | | X | 90 | X | | | X | X |
| 14 SALT RIVER CANYON | 3000 | All Yr. | | X | 24 | | | | | X |
| 15 SHUSH BE TOU LAKE | 7500 | All Yr. | | X | | X | | | X | X |
| 16 SHUSH BE ZAHZE LAKE | 7500 | All Yr. | | X | 20 | | | | X | X |
| 17 SUNRISE LAKE | 9200 | All Yr. | | X | 200 | X | | | X | X |
| 18 UPPER LOG ROAD | 6500 | All Yr. | | X | 95 | | | | | X |

# Campsites

There are restrooms, table-bench units, and a water supply. A year-round store is a bonus. Elevation is a cool 8500 feet.

**Ditch Camp** lies along the North Fork of the White River, just off State Route 260 about 15 miles east of McNary. There are 35 sites, about half with table-bench units and restrooms. No drinking water.

**McCoy Bridge** campground is on State Route 473, the Hawley Lake road, just after the turnoff from Route 260. The sites are found both upstream and downstream along the North Fork; some have table-bench units, others space for a recreational vehicle. Restrooms; no drinking water.

**Sunrise Lake** is reached by turning off State Route 273 at the Sunrise service station and heading toward the ski complex. The campground access road is on the left, 100 yards or so off the pavement. There are approximately 200 sites, spread out along a ridge about a half-mile from the lake. Thick timber and widely dispersed sites make it seem uncrowded even when other campers are nearby. Table-bench units; restrooms; water faucets at several locations. A hotel with a restaurant is on the main highway. The 9200-foot elevation makes for perfect summertime sleeping.

**Reservation Lake** has one big campground on a thickly forested ridge above the lake, just off the access road as you approach from Big Lake; another near the spillway crossing; and some scattered sites along the lake's shoreline in other areas. These last have no facilities and are intended for self-contained campers. Drinking water; restrooms; table-bench units at most sites. In summer, a store provides picnic supplies, ice, fishing tackle, rental boats. Reservation Lake is almost never filled to capacity. There are 90 sites in all.

*(Right) The White River is one of two "mother" streams (the Black is the other) that drain most of the Apache high country. There are campgrounds at many places along its length. Jerry Jacka*
*(Below) Reservation temperatures can be nippy even during the summer months, and a fire feels good early and late in the day. Tom Bean*

**Drift Fence Lake** campground is very casual, with sites on two sides of the small lake. Restroom; some table-bench units, no drinking water.

**Pacheta Lake** always has room for campers. Some of the 25 sites have table-bench units. Restrooms; no drinking water.

**East Fork,** the campground on the White River, consists of about 12 sites scattered along the river banks east of the town of Whiteriver. No drinking water. Restroom; but most sites are for recreational vehicles and self-contained campers.

**Diamond Creek** has miniclusters of campsites along its course over a distance of 20 miles. Although there is no drinking water, restrooms and tables are available wherever several sites are clustered. There are about 25 sites in all.

**Cibecue Creek** campground comprises 10 sites along the creek north of the town of Cibecue. Very casual. Restroom; table-bench units. No drinking water.

**Salt River Canyon** is a good fall, winter, or spring campground downstream from the U. S. Route 60 bridge at the bottom of the Salt River Canyon. There are about 24 sites along the river. Restroom; table-bench units. No drinking water. The surroundings are spectacular. Elevation is 3000 feet. Store open all year sells food, gas, fishing tackle and camping supplies.

# Central Arizona

Many Arizonans are rabid outdoors enthusiasts. This is abundantly clear in the Phoenix area every Friday afternoon, when a steady stream of cars, trailers, pickups, and motor homes heads out of town for a weekend in the open air. Destinations vary according to time of the year, but thousands of these solace-seekers are dreaming of a campsite in the scenic desert near Phoenix or in the pines and oaks of the Tonto National Forest north and east of the valley communities. Campers from other parts of Arizona also enjoy this section of the state, of course, but it is particularly popular with Phoenicians, who consider it their own huge backyard playground.

Most of the desert camping is water-oriented, close to one of the reservoirs of the Salt, Verde, or Agua Fria rivers — all built to store water for irrigation and power generation. Spring and early summer used to be the camping times on the lakes, but nowadays

Laurie G. Kriz

villages of recreational vehicles and tents blossom every weekend at Roosevelt, Apache, Canyon, and the rest of the lakes. If it's too cold to swim, water ski, or sunbathe, the campers fish, hunt, sail, or cruise. Only during the coldest, rain-filled days do Lake Pleasant, Bartlett, Horseshoe, Saguaro, and the other lakes look nearly deserted. A balmy spring weekend at Roosevelt can mean 15,000 sun worshipers, a small city of tent-stake pounders and recreational vehicle levelers, all intent on claiming a stretch of lakeshore and a share of the brilliant sunshine.

There is pine country in this region, too — especially in the Sierra Ancha range, high above Roosevelt Lake

and the Tonto Basin, and in the Pinals, the massive mountains that loom above Globe and Miami. The vast views from the top of the Pinals are well worth the winding drive up the flanks of the range, and the small, colorful campgrounds you encounter are a valuable fringe benefit.

Phoenix and the surrounding area furnish numerous sharp contrasts. Up in Bloody Basin, a few miles north of Bartlett and Horseshoe reservoirs — still within sight of the lights that fill the valley after sunset — begins some of the wildest, most rugged country in the Southwest. Only a few dirt roads wind through its interior, and four-wheel-drive side trails labor up and down to old mine operations or remote cattle tanks. There are no improved campgrounds, and in summer the chaparral-covered hills bake in the sun. But the rest of the year is different. Hidden groves of sycamore and ash trees form shady tunnels along the slender streams that flow in late winter and spring in some of the rocky canyons.

All this lonesome country offers camping opportunities to the adventuresome. An hour away from the center of Phoenix you can set up camp under a canopy of trees and settle in — alone for as long as you care to be.

This same kind of solitude is easy to find in the Sierra Ancha, away from State Route 288's path along the mountains' crest. You'll likely need a four-wheel-drive vehicle to negotiate the narrow, rocky roads. But some unique camping spots await, including places along Cherry Creek that are private enough that you can skinny-dip in some of the deeper pools. And all through this country are Indian ruins, remains of cliff dwellings in the steep canyons, evidence that others chose this part of Arizona more than a thousand years ago.

So those outdoor fans who flee to the hills every Friday can choose the kind of camping they like best. Maybe a lakefront villa (of canvas) at Horse Pasture on the Tonto arm of Roosevelt Lake; or a mountain view from the window of their recreational vehicle at Tortilla Flat; or a guaranteed "No Solicitors" site in Bloody Basin's chaparral. It's all Arizona, and it's all delightful.

*(Right) Eternal stars and an ancient saguaro testify to the fleeting moments of time represented by this campsite on the Arizona desert. Richard D. Fisher*

*(Above) One more cup before bedtime. Rick O'Dell*
*(Right) Tortilla campground, along the Apache Trail beyond Canyon Lake, is perfect during fall, winter, and spring months, when the desert is in a welcoming mood. Jerry Sieve*
*(Below) Fish Creek murmurs its sweet desert song beside the Apache Trail. David Muench*

(Above) Lost Dutchman State Park is at the foot of the Superstition Mountains. No gold, just camping beside a legend. James Tallon
(Left) Canyon Lake on the Salt River, a blue oasis in the rugged desert landscape. David Muench
(Below) Trolling from an early version of a bass boat. Dick Dietrich

(Above) A bobcat takes an evening drink. Desert
creatures are most active after the sun goes down.
Laurie Kriz
(Right) Roosevelt is the grandaddy of the Salt River chain
of lakes. It hosts hundreds of recreational vehicles along its
shore on pleasant spring weekends. Lon McAdam
(Below) Apache Lake is well named: Indians used the
surrounding canyons as hiding places after raids in the
Tonto Basin. There are two campgrounds here.
Bob Hirsch

# James Ohio Pattie
## Arizona's Pioneer Storyteller

**Around the Campfire**

The first Anglo-Americans to penetrate the rugged wilderness regions of Arizona were a reckless breed known as the mountain men. Prior to the explorations by these hardy trappers in the 1820s, few people east of "the wide Missouri" were even aware of the vast uncharted lands that some forty years later would be called Arizona.

The earliest written account was the narrative of James Ohio Pattie of Kentucky. Pattie's bigger-than-life story reads like a cross between pulp fiction and stage melodrama. He braved Comanche lances to rescue women and fought grizzlies, mountain lions, and Apaches.

James Pattie arrived in Santa Fe in the fall of 1825. It was the heyday of the fur trade, and he was bound for the pristine hunting grounds of the Gila River country. The Gila watershed was an untapped resource of beaver pelts or "hairy bank notes", back in the days when beaver hats were in fashion and commerce in pelts was one of America's great economic enterprises. The Southwest was still part of the Republic of Mexico, however, and the Mexicans weren't eager to see the increasing number of rough-hewn, buckskin-clad Americans, who were setting up business in Taos and Santa Fe.

For that reason, the twenty-year-old Kentuckian was delayed in Santa Fe when he tried to secure a Mexican license. Governor Antonio Narbona might never have granted the license had fate not intervened in a most dramatic way.

A Comanche war party swooped down on Santa Fe and carried off some young women. Pattie, outraged at such barbaric behavior, joined a punitive expedition that dashed off in hot pursuit. The party ambushed the Comanches a few miles away, and Pattie made a daring rescue of one of the captives. During the fighting our hero rode in and scooped up a beautiful damsel in distress named Jacova. The ladies had been stripped of nearly all their clothing, so Pattie removed his buckskin jacket, gallantly place it over Jacova's bare shoulders, and then returned her safely to Santa Fe.

It turned out that Jacova was the governor's daughter. Needless to say, the grateful official had a change of heart, and the American was granted a license to go trapping in Gila country.

During the next couple of years Pattie trapped along the river and its tributaries, accumulating enough adventures to write a dime novel. One morning, for example, he came upon a dark cave. With the recklessness of youth, Pattie rigged a pine torch to the end of his rifle and entered the cave, only to come face to face with a huge grizzly she-bear. Pattie aimed his rifle at the shadowy figure and fired. Without waiting to see if the shot was on target, he turned and made a hasty exit, dropping his rifle along the way. Moments later, his courage regained, he borrowed another rifle and reentered the cave. The critter was sprawled out dead on the floor. Pattie declared that it took four men to haul the carcass out.

On another occasion, one morning, a mountain lion nearly did him in. When Pattie awakened, the beast was perched on a log less than six feet from his bedroll and was preparing to leap. Pattie grabbed his rifle and fired point blank, killing the animal with a head shot.

In the fall of 1826, Pattie joined a party of French trappers led by Michel Robidoux and journeyed down the Gila to the junction of the Salt and Gila rivers (near where Avondale stands today). The Frenchmen planned to spend a night of frivolous activity in a native village. Pattie, suspicious, decided to camp a safe distance away. During the night he was awakened by the sounds of a deadly struggle. A short time later Robidoux and another trapper staggered into Pattie's camp to report the Indians had attacked and all the others were dead.

The three survivors traveled upstream (presumably through what today is downtown Phoenix), and by sheer luck chanced upon another party of trappers led by the famed mountain man Ewing Young. Next day the vengeful trappers returned to the scene of the massacre, gave the Indians a sound thrashing, and burned their village. Afterwards they gathered the scattered remains of the Frenchmen and buried them.

A few weeks later, while camped on the Colorado River, Pattie miraculously escaped injury during another attack, when a war party of Mohaves launched a shower of arrows into the trappers' camp. The next morning he discovered his bedroll was punctured by sixteen arrows.

Pattie remained with Young's outfit the rest of the season. They trapped up and down the Salt and Verde rivers, then followed the Gila to the Yuma crossing to become the first Anglos to follow the Gila all the way to its mouth.

James Pattie remained in the Southwest and continued trapping along the Verde and Salt rivers, but bad luck plagued him. Despite the abundance of beaver and his successful hunts, it seemed all too often that if the Apaches didn't steal his furs, the Mexican authorities confiscated them.

In the mid-1830s, an older and wiser Pattie returned to his old Kentucky home. Discouraged, weary, and broke, he summed up his Arizona adventure with this lament: "The freshness, the visions, the hopes of my youthful days are all vanished, and can never return."

Pattie didn't keep a journal of his Western travels but rather relied on recall, telling his story to the Reverend Timothy Flint, who edited it for publication. It makes for interesting reading.

It was customary for the mountain men to stretch their tales a bit, and doubtless Pattie was no exception. Still, there was a sound basis of fact underlying his colorful accounts, and he has provided his readers with an important piece of history of the fur trade in Arizona.

**Campfire Recipes**

### BAKED APPLE SURPRISE

Core an apple, set it on a square of foil and fill the cavity with a mixture of cinnamon and sugar. Wrap the apple in the foil and bake in the oven, campfire, or on the grill. Turn several times on the grill or in the coals. Just fifteen minutes to sweet dessert.

## CRAWDAD SPECIALTIES

Crayfish (also known as crawdads) are found in nearly all Arizona lakes. You can use a trap to gather a large number in a short time, or simply dunk a bit of bacon on a fish line and slowly lift the clinging crawdad from the water. Save the largest (some qualify as mini-lobsters) and cook for happy-hour treats, salad makings, or any other recipe that calls for shrimp. Most markets have bags of spices (usually called crab or crawdad boil), or you can just use salted boiling water.

Rinse the crayfish in fresh water and pop into rapidly boiling water for eight to ten minutes. They will turn bright red, exactly like lobsters. Remove from water and let cool. There is some meat in the claws, but most are too small to bother with; concentrate on the tail. Pop it off the body, peel as you would a shrimp, and remove the dark vein. It's ready to serve.

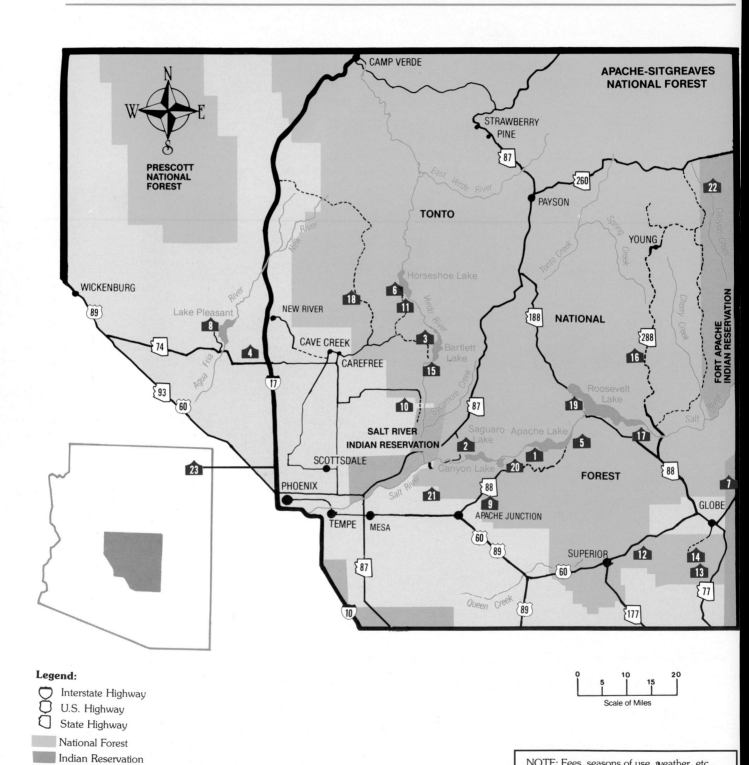

APACHE-SITGREAVES
NATIONAL FOREST

PRESCOTT
NATIONAL
FOREST

TONTO

NATIONAL

FOREST

FORT APACHE
INDIAN RESERVATION

SALT RIVER
INDIAN RESERVATION

CAMP VERDE

STRAWBERRY
PINE

PAYSON

YOUNG

WICKENBURG

NEW RIVER

CAVE CREEK

CAREFREE

SCOTTSDALE

PHOENIX

TEMPE

MESA

APACHE JUNCTION

SUPERIOR

GLOBE

Horseshoe Lake

Bartlett Lake

Saguaro Lake

Apache Lake

Canyon Lake

Roosevelt Lake

Lake Pleasant

Salt River

Queen Creek

**Legend:**

Interstate Highway

U.S. Highway

State Highway

National Forest

Indian Reservation

Campsite

0    5    10    15    20

Scale of Miles

NOTE: Fees, seasons of use, weather, etc., can cause changes in the availability of camping facilities. For updated information on this region, see agency addresses and phone numbers listed inside the back cover.

# Central Arizona Campsites

**Rose Creek** campground, small but delightful, has only 5 sites. They are widely separated, and the area offers a textbook display of native trees and shrubs. Rose Creek is at 5400 feet, on the crest of the Sierra Ancha mountain range, just off State Route 288 — the road that links Roosevelt Lake and Young. No fee. Water supply; 14-day stay limit. No room for large recreational vehicles; trailers limited to 16 feet or less. The campground is open from May to November, and is seldom full. Don't forget to bring a tree identification guide.

**Valentine Ridge** is a 9-unit campground near Canyon Creek. The small stream is full of trout; overhead looms the Mogollon Rim. No drinking water; no fee; 14-day stay limit. Elevation is 6500 feet, and the season is May-November. Access is via State Route 288 (the Young road), for about 3 miles south of State Route 260 atop the Rim, then 3 miles east on Forest Road 188. Tonto National Forest officials advise against trailers of more than 16 feet in length.

**Tonto arm of Roosevelt Lake** has no fully developed campgrounds along the western shore, but there are enough campers here from late winter to early summer to populate a small town. Tonto National Forest has provided outhouses and garbage bins along the shore. There's a paved launch ramp and parking area at Cholla, about 9 miles northwest of Roosevelt Dam, and a do-it-yourself launch area at Bermuda Flat. Do-it-yourself dispersed camping areas begin at Bachelor Cove, about 7 miles north of the dam off State Route 188.

Except for Bermuda Flat, these areas are normally open all year, with a 14-day stay limit. There's no source of drinking water. Elevation is 2100 feet. How much camping space is available depends on the lake's water level. Mesquite trees provide shade for early comers. It's not fancy, or even pretty, but you are close to the water.

**Salt River arm of Roosevelt Lake** has a store, service station, marina, and ranger station on State Route 88 about 2 miles east of the dam. There is a paved boat-launch ramp at the marina. Camping at this end of the lake is not quite as dispersed as on the Tonto arm, but otherwise follows the same pattern. The Porter Springs and Windy Hill areas are about 5 miles from the small community of Roosevelt; about half the distance is via paved State Route 88 and the rest by unimproved dirt road. Windy Hill has 2 paved launch ramps, and the 2 areas share a dump station

for recreational vehicle holding tanks. No fee; no potable water. Outhouses and garbage bins provided. Elevation is 2100 feet; 14-day stay limit is in effect.

The next area east along the lakeshore is Grapevine — about 4 paved miles past Windy Hill, then 2.5 miles north to the lake. It has dispersed camping and an unimproved boat launch. Schoolhouse Point is about a mile east of the turnoff to Grapevine, then

| | RECREATION SITE NAME | APPROX. ELEV. | SEASONS OF USE | DAYS-LIMITS | FEE | NO. OF UNITS | SAFE WATER | 16 FT. RV LIMIT | WASTE DISP. | BOATING | FISHING |
|---|---|---|---|---|---|---|---|---|---|---|---|
| 1 | APACHE LAKE | 1900 | All Yr. | 14 | | 12 | | X | | X | X |
| 2 | BAGLEY FLAT | 1500 | All Yr. | 14 | | 30 | | | | X | X |
| 3 | BARTLETT LAKE | 1900 | All Yr. | 14 | | | | | | X | X |
| 4 | BLACK CANYON Shooting Range | 1400 | All Yr. | 14 | X | 100 | X | | X | | |
| 5 | BURNT CORRAL | 1800 | All Yr. | 14 | | 17 | X | | | X | X |
| 6 | HORSESHOE | 1900 | All yr. | 14 | | 8 | X | | | X | X |
| 7 | JONES WATER | 4500 | All Yr. | 14 | | 12 | | | | | |
| 8 | LAKE PLEASANT (Dirty Shirt) | 1600 | All Yr. | 3 | X | 46 | | | | X | X |
| 9 | LOST DUTCHMAN | 1700 | All Yr. | 14 | X | 35 | X | | X | | |
| 10 | McDOWELL Mtn. REGIONAL PARK | 2000 | All Yr. | 14 | X | 40 | X | | X | | |
| 11 | MESQUITE | 1900 | All Yr. | 14 | | 100 | | | | | X |
| 12 | OAK FLAT | 4200 | All Yr. | 14 | | 16 | X | | | | |
| 13 | PINAL & UPPER PINAL | 7500 | May Nov. | 14 | | 15 | X | X | | | |
| 14 | PIONEER PASS | 6000 | Apr. Dec. | 14 | | 27 | X | | | | |
| 15 | RIVERSIDE | 1600 | All Yr. | 14 | | 8 | | | | | X |
| 16 | ROSE CREEK | 5400 | May Nov. | 14 | | 5 | X | X | | | |
| 17 | SALT RIVER ARM Of Roosevelt Lake | 2100 | All Yr. | 14 | | | | | X | X | X |
| 18 | SEVEN SPRINGS | 3400 | All Yr. | 14 | | 23 | X | | | | |
| 19 | TONTO ARM Of Roosevelt Lake | 2100 | All Yr. | 14 | | | | | | X | X |
| 20 | TORTILLA | 1800 | Oct. Apr. | 14 | X | 77 | X | | X | X | X |
| 21 | USERY MTN. REGIONAL PARK | 2000 | All Yr. | 14 | X | 75 | X | | X | | |
| 22 | VALENTINE RIDGE | 6500 | May Nov. | 14 | | 9 | X | | | | X |
| 23 | WHITE TANKS | 1500 | All Yr. | 14 | X | 40 | X | | | | |

# Campsites

about 4 miles by dirt road to the lake. There is an unimproved launch area here.

**Apache Lake** is the next reservoir southwest along the Salt River. The campground is just up the shoreline from the marina, so you're close to a motel, trailer park, cafe, and bar. There are 12 sites in the campground, but no water. No fee. Elevation is 1900 feet; the area is open all year. This one is always full during the spring and summer. Trailers over 16 feet are not allowed. Access road turns off State Route 88—the Apache Trail—about 32 miles northeast of Apache Junction. The first 18 miles of the famed Trail are smooth, though winding, pavement; the rest is gravel and includes the notorious Fish Creek Hill.

**Burnt Corral** is Apache's other campground, a mile off the highway about 8 miles north of the marina—approximately halfway from Apache Marina to Roosevelt Dam. There are 17 sites here, suitable for tents, campers, and trailers up to 16 feet. No fee; no water; stay limit, 14 days. Open all year. Table-bench units; Forest Service outhouses. Paved boat launch; swimming area. This location is very popular from March to June, but after that the hot weather tends to discourage visitors until fall.

**Tortilla** has 77 campsites set on 3 levels, just above the spot where Tortilla Creek empties into Canyon Lake. The campground was designed with trailers and motor homes in mind. Each site is a concrete slab with sewer outlet and water hookup. Modern restrooms serve the complex. Fee; 14-day stay limit; dump station for holding tanks. Elevation is only 1800 feet. The campground is closed from May 1-September 30.

**Lost Dutchman State Park** is just off State Route 88 (The Apache Trail) a few miles northeast of Apache Junction. There are 35 campsites here, both pull-throughs and back-ins, laid out in a large loop in the lush desert. The steep western face of the Superstition Mountain range looms over the campground. There are water taps and restrooms at several locations in the campground and a dump station near the entrance. The park is open all year, with spring, fall and winter months most popular. The stay-limit is 14 days, and a fee is charged. A major trail system into the Tonto National Forest wilderness area begins here.

**McDowell Mountain Regional Park**, 15 miles northeast of Scottsdale, is a whisper away from civilization. The 40-unit campground also has a large trailhead for group camping. This Maricopa County park has water and electricity hookups, modern shower and restroom facilities, hiking and riding trails, and table-bench-grill units. Fee; 14-day stay limit; 72-hour limit for groups. Elevation is 2,000 feet.

**Bagley Flat** is Saguaro Lake's only entry in the camping derby. Bagley Flat is a boat-access facility on the southern shore of the lake, up past Shiprock. There are 30 sites sprinkled along the sloping beach. You can put your boat's bow on land and pitch a tent, or, in good weather, simply lay out a ground cloth and unroll your sleeping bag. There are table-bench units and outhouses. The campground is open all year; stay limit is 14 days. No fee; no drinking water. Elevation is 1500 feet.

**Usery Mountain Regional Park,** also a Maricopa County park, is 12 miles from central Mesa off Usery Pass at Ellsworth Road. Both the 75-unit campground and group camping area have water and electrical hookups, modern restroom and shower facilities, and table-bench units. A horse staging area, riding and hiking trails, and archery range cater to campers' special interests. Though open all year, the campsite fills with winter visitors from October through March. Fee; 14-day stay limit; 72-hour limit for groups. Elevation is 2,000 feet.

**Seven Springs** is a mini-oasis in the chaparral desert that surrounds it. The campground is set amid tall ash and sycamore trees about 20 miles northeast of Cave Creek and Carefree. There are 23 sites on a narrow bench above a small stream, with just enough water to get the dog and kids wet. No fee; no potable water; 14-day stay limit. Open all year. Elevation is 3400 feet, so in summer it is appreciably cooler than the Salt River Valley below, and the big trees provide a pleasant canopy of shade. Take the paved road east from Carefree past the turnoff to Bartlett Lake, then follow Forest Road 24 (usually bumpy and dusty) to the campground. Maneuvering room is limited; motor homes and trailers longer than 16 feet are not recommended.

**Horseshoe** campground is on a bench above the Verde River, just downstream from Horseshoe Dam. It's worth the rough, dusty drive just to see the massive mesquite trees that shade the 8 sites. But the trees do cause problems for tall recreational vehicles, and space is tight, so smaller rigs are best. No fee; no water; 14-day stay limit. Open all year. Elevation is only 1900 feet, so summer temperatures soar. Horseshoe is 23 miles northeast of Carefree via Forest roads

24 and 205—about 11 miles are unpaved. Trailers longer than 16 feet are discouraged.

**Mesquite** is a half-mile downstream from Horseshoe. Its approximately 100 primitive sites are nestled among a miniature forest of mesquite trees. No fee; no water; outhouses; 14-day stay limit. Elevation is 1900 feet. The campground is open all year.

**Bartlett Lake** has several minimally developed campgrounds, including South Cove, Rattlesnake, S.B. Cove, and Bartlett Flats. Though crowded during the summer, these campsites are ideal for more relaxed fall and spring camping. Jojoba, the lake's paved boat launch site, is targeted for further improvement. The campsites, open all year, are east of Carefree via Forest Roads 24, 205, and 19. No fee; 14-day stay limit; outhouses.

**Riverside** campground is on the Verde River a few miles south of Bartlett Lake's Jojoba boating site. There is shade from cottonwood and mesquite trees. When Salt River Project releases water into the Verde, canoeing, rafting and tubing are allowed. The 8-unit unimproved campground is open all year. No fee; 14-day stay limit; outhouses. Elevation: 1600 feet.

**Lake Pleasant**, northwest of Phoenix off State Route 74, is one of the most popular camping, fishing, and boating areas in the state. The 46-unit campground on the western side of the lake is called **Dirty Shirt**. Concrete table-bench units; fire rings; flush toilets. No drinking water. The campground is on a point stretching to the water, and it's possible to launch smaller boats from here. There are small bushes but no shade, and elevation is only 1600 feet, so summer temperatures are very warm. Entrance fee for the park; additional fee to camp. Maricopa County, the landlord, enforces a 72-hour time limit on camping.

**White Tanks** is also Maricopa County property. Set on the flank of the mountain range of the same name, the park features a huge picnic area and a 40-unit campground with table-bench units, standup grills, and restrooms. Some sites have electricity and water hookups. The park is open all year, but the low elevation (about 1500 feet) means summer months are very warm. There's a large group-camping area, available by reservation, with a stay limit of 72 hours; otherwise the stay limit is 2 weeks. There is a fee. Access is via Olive Avenue 15 miles west of Peoria. It's possible to park your recreational vehicle here.

**Oak Flat** has oaks, but the country is gently rolling rather than flat. This Tonto National Forest campground is just off U.S. Route 60, 4 miles east of Superior. No fee; no water; 16 sites; 14-day stay limit. Trailers limited to 16 feet. Open all year. Elevation is 4200 feet.

**Jones Water** campground is tucked away in a tree-filled canyon beside busy U.S. Route 60, 17 miles north of Globe. There are 12 sites and room for a few additional, self-contained recreational vehicles. No fee; no water; table-bench units; outhouse. Stay limit, 14 days. Open year-round. Elevation is 4500 feet.

**Pioneer Pass** is on an upper flank of the Pinal Mountains, the huge, bulky range that looms above the Globe-Miami area. The 9-mile drive from Globe is mostly uphill on Forest Road 112, a gentle ascent with views improving as each mile passes. No fee; 27 campsites; water; 14-day stay limit. Elevation is 6000 feet, and the season is April to December. Water is turned off during the colder months when there is a threat of freezing. Trailers are limited to 16 feet.

**Pinal** campground and its sister facility, **Upper Pinal**, are a mile apart and nearly at the top of the highest feature in the Pinal Mountains, Signal Peak. The Army stationed a heliograph here in territorial days, flashing messages to other high points to the south and east. Both campgrounds are at 7500 feet. Pinal has 10 sites; Upper Pinal, 5. No fee; 14-day stay limits; May-November season. The water supply is turned off in the colder months. Take it easy on the narrow, winding road that climbs the 15 miles from Globe (large recreational vehicles may have problems). Take Forest Road 112, then follow the signs.

**Black Canyon Shooting Range** is just off Interstate 17 about 23 miles north of Phoenix. Take the Carefree Highway-Lake Pleasant-Shooting Range exit. The entrance to this Maricopa County park campground is on the left as you enter the Shooting Range complex. The 100 sites are laid out in loops in the desert terrain. Fifty-four of the back-in sites have electric and water hookups; the remaining do not, although a few do have water available. Daily or weekly fees vary according to the amenities at the site. Nearby are restroom buildings that include hot showers; there is a dump station, telephones, and public fire rings (ground fires are otherwise prohibited). There's a 2-week stay limit and the campground is open all year, though summertime temperatures are hot.

# The San Carlos Reservation

The domain of the San Carlos Apache is big—nearly two million acres big. Away from the communities clustered along U.S. Route 70, great chunks of the back country have little or no access for the casual visitor. In fact, except for an occasional cowboy or hunter, many of the dim, two-track roads get no traffic from one year to the next. Off the paved highways, even the so-called main roads can be an adventure; they're mostly suitable for pickup trucks or other high-clearance vehicles. The side roads usually lead to dirt tanks—watering holes for cattle—built by the same bulldozer that scraped out a road to the site. That may have been twenty years ago, and little or no maintenance has been done since. So these rocky, twisting trails, following the path of least resistance, are sometimes impassable even to a four-wheel-drive vehicle, unless a little on-the-spot road improvement is done.

Most visitors stick with the easy access along the shoreline of San Carlos Lake, the big reservoir on the Gila River south of the community of San Carlos, headquarters of the San Carlos Apache Tribe. Or they head for the broad, forested plateau atop the Nantac Rim, along the northern quarter of the reservation, where the stock ponds have been planted with rainbow trout or channel catfish. Here many of the campers are also anglers who appreciate the opportunity to get away from crowds.

There are some ramadas, trash barrels, and outhouses at the most popular launching areas on San Carlos Lake, and the Apache have upgraded facilities and road signs around the lake. Regular garbage collection schedules have helped a lot, too. Still, campers here need to be more or less self-sufficient. Elevation at the lake is about 2500 feet, so summer temperatures often go above the 100-degree mark.

Compare that with the coolness of Malay Gap, in the northeastern part of the reservation, where the elevation is more than 8000 feet. Except for an accessible campground at Point of Pines Lake in the high country, there are no facilities in this area. But there are lots of pine trees for shade, lots of rough roads, and lots of quiet solitude. Apache Route 10 begins at U.S. Route 60 north of Globe and runs across the reservation's wooded plateau for more than a hundred miles. There are a number of stock ponds—some several acres in size—along this road, and stub roads lead north and south to other, smaller tanks. You'll find no towns along this route, no gas stations, no supplies, no drinking water, no telephones; indeed, no other people most of the time. Campers who spend a few days in this huge, unpopulated area have a good chance to sight deer, bear, turkey, and squirrel. And there's always a coyote chorus to sing you to sleep at night.

The northern border of the reservation is the Black River, the dividing line between the lands of the San Carlos Apache and White Mountain Apache tribes. The Black holds trout in its upper reaches, smallmouth bass and channel catfish in the warmer sections. Only one road goes to the stream from the San Carlos side: Apache Route 9. The rest of the river is a hike-in destination.

So the San Carlos is an immense, largely undeveloped outdoor playground. It is not for the faint of heart nor the ill-equipped. But you are welcome to enjoy its wild beauty, and if you fancy camping where no one has ever camped, where a tent peg has never been driven or a campfire lit, there are hundreds of such places here for you.

*(Above left) Camping facilities are minimal at San Carlos Lake. There are a few ramadas, some tables, trash barrels, but most campers are self-contained. Ken Akers (Right) It's the excellent fishing that draws the most campers to San Carlos Lake. The dam that impounds the lake is named after President Calvin Coolidge, who made a speech at its dedication. Ken Akers*

(Clockwise, from right) *Hint of a summer afternoon
shower.* Ken Akers
*A bold camp visitor.* Dick Dietrich
*Cattail pollen spreads to the wind.* Wes Holden
*Settin' up camp in time for supper.* J. Peter Mortimer
*The Nantac Rim divides the San Carlos Apache
Reservation from grassland to high pine plateau.*
Jerry Jacka
*Point of Pines Lake has one of the few developed
campgrounds on the San Carlos reservation.*
J. Peter Mortimer

# "If That Was My Lake I'd Mow It"

## Around the Campfire

One of the many things that strike newcomers as peculiar about Arizona is our insistence on referring to dry streambeds as rivers.

Just the other day, a tourist said to me, "Sir, your creeks have more running water than your rivers."

Well, he had me there; but I went on to point out the advantages of catching native desert trout in the Rio Seco (dry river). "They're already fried and ready to eat when you catch 'em," I explained. "The only trouble is that when you try to hook 'em, they've been known to kick dust in your face." His curiosity suitably aroused, I solemnly continued: "An old-timer up at Globe told me about a flash flood that drowned a whole species of native trout."

The damming of Arizona's great rivers has made their channels mere traces of the old turbulent days. Still, those irreverent streams are quite capable of kicking off their hobbles and running wild like a spring colt.

Personally, my favorite river is the Gila. Its Spanish name translates roughly as "a steady going to or coming from" someplace. And that's what the old river did for several thousand years, though, today it is one of our driest rivers. Before it was dammed, it meandered across Arizona, sustaining a rich lifestyle for the Pima Indians, and before that for the prehistoric Hohokam. In time Spanish missionaries and soldiers camped on its banks, and Mexican vaqueros gathered wild cattle on its brushy floodplain.

During the California gold rush, would-be millionaires on their way to the promised land used to float down the Gila, saving themselves the hazards crossing the fearsome desert sands.

It has been said that in 1849 a Mrs. Howard gave birth to a baby boy while traveling down the Gila on a raft. He was named "Gila" in honor of his birthplace, and the folklore has it that he was the first Anglo child born within the boundaries of what would become Arizona.

Three years earlier, Lieutenant George Stoneman of the famed Mormon Battalion experimented with transporting military goods on the Gila. The raft, with Stoneman on board, was launched amid as much ceremony as one could manage in the wilds of Arizona. A short distance downstream the raft began to sink, and Lieutenant Stoneman, a brave sea captain to the end, went down with his ship—then walked ashore. As far as we know, that was the last time there was any government-sponsored navigation on the Gila.

Wet years and dry came in their cycles, just as they had for countless centuries, and the venerable Gila continued to go its own way in its own time.

In 1885, the Thirteenth Territorial Legislature appropriated $1200 to build a bridge across the Gila. The citizens of Florence were tired of the river's fickle behavior.

No sooner had the bridge been built and dedicated than the irrepressible Gila changed its course, swung out into the desert, and left the new bridge standing all alone.

In 1930 the U.S. Bureau of Reclamation completed the construction of Coolidge Dam on the upper Gila. The bureau had researched the river thoroughly before deciding where the dam should be built. Unfortunately, however, the years reviewed in the study were unusually wet—and a series of years after the dam was finished were unusually dry. Well, the Gila got stubborn and refused to form the reservoir that was supposed to take shape behind the dam. It took fifty years, in fact, for San Carlos Lake to fill.

Will Rogers, at the dedication ceremony attended by President Coolidge in 1930, looked at the grassy lake bed and said, "If that was my lake, I'd mow it."

## Campfire Recipes

### STEW IS NUMBER ONE

Stew has always been the camper's standby. You can make it in camp with whatever ingredients are available; but it's easier to make it at home, freeze it, then thaw and heat in camp for the supreme one-dish meal. This version for an electric slow-cooking pot is delicious:

Dice 6 slices of bacon and brown in a pan; remove and let drain. Using the same bacon-greased pan, brown cubes of meat (about 3 pounds); salt and pepper to taste. Put the meat and bacon in the pot, and use the pan again to brown 3 large carrots, sliced, and a medium onion, diced. Add 2 10-ounce cans condensed beef broth, and thicken with flour. Then add 1 teaspoon thyme; 4 cloves garlic, minced; 1 bay leaf; 1 jar white onions; and 2 small cans tomato sauce. (A can of diced potatoes is optional, it will thicken the stew.)

Put all ingredients in the electric pot and cook for 8 to 10 hours on low setting or 3 to 4 hours on high. In the last hour, add about 3/4 pound to 1 pound sliced fresh mushrooms, browned, and 1 cup of burgundy wine.

Serve with garlic bread you have wrapped in foil and heated by the campfire.

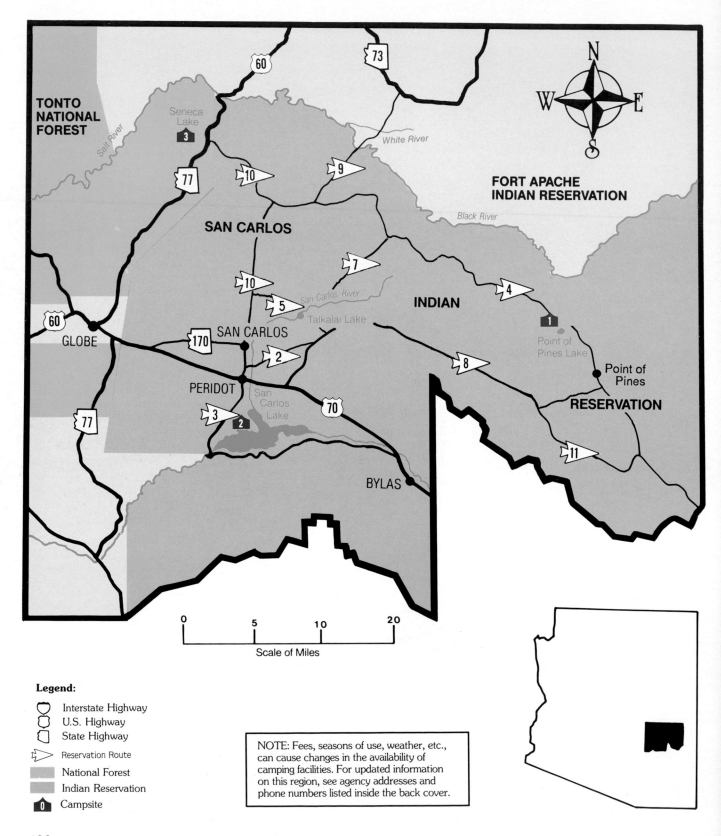

**60** **73**

**TONTO NATIONAL FOREST**

Salt River

Seneca Lake

**3**

White River

**77**

**10** **9**

**SAN CARLOS**

**FORT APACHE INDIAN RESERVATION**

Black River

**7**

**10** **4**

**5**

San Carlos River

**INDIAN**

**1**

Talkalai Lake

Point of Pines Lake

**60**

**GLOBE**

**170** **SAN CARLOS**

**2**

**8**

Point of Pines

**PERIDOT**

San Carlos Lake

**70**

**RESERVATION**

**3**

**2**

**77**

**11**

**BYLAS**

N
W E
S

Scale of Miles

0    5    10    20

**Legend:**

Interstate Highway
U.S. Highway
State Highway
Reservation Route
National Forest
Indian Reservation
**0** Campsite

NOTE: Fees, seasons of use, weather, etc., can cause changes in the availability of camping facilities. For updated information on this region, see agency addresses and phone numbers listed inside the back cover.

# San Carlos Apache Campsites

The San Carlos Game and Fish Department previously only charged fees for camping at its 2 developed sites, Point of Pines Lake and Seneca Lake. But now a fee is charged to camp anywhere on San Carlos land. Contact the department for fee information on camping, boating, and fishing.

**San Carlos Lake** has only primitive accommodations, but there is ample opportunity for hundreds of campers to select campsites on or near its banks. The lake, 20 miles east of Globe and 7 miles south on a marked paved road, lures anglers with an abundance of bass, crappie, catfish, and bluegills. There is no water or waste disposal, but there are a few outhouses, table-bench units and picnic ramadas, which are handy at a shadeless desert elevation of 2800 feet. Open all year; no stay limit; fee. There is no improved launch ramp, but the large lake can accommodate a fleet of boats. Permits, gas and groceries can be purchased at the Lake's store.

**Point of Pines Lake** is just west of the tiny community of the same name, in the eastern part of the reservation. Access is via Apache Route 8 to Point of Pines (38 miles are paved plus 14 miles of gravel), then west about 5 miles to the lake and campground. Eighteen sites are scattered among the pines near the lake, each with a table-bench unit. There are pit toilets. This campground is seldom crowded. Visitors are restricted by the high-clearance vehicle requirement, and the lake is a long way from the state's population centers. Elevation is about 6500 feet, so spring, summer, and fall months are pleasant. The campground is open year-round, but snow limits access during the December-March period. There is a 14-day stay limit, and a fee is charged. The lake is well stocked with rainbow trout; catching enough fish for lunch is not difficult.

**Seneca Lake** is the San Carlos Apache's other developed campground. There are 40 sites here. Camping and fishing permits (a small lake contains trout, bass, catfish, and bluegills) are sold at a tribe convenience store/gas station on U.S. Route 60. Seneca Lake is a pleasant, shady spot but campers need to be completely self-contained. The campground is just west of U.S. Route 60, about 32 miles north of Globe. The lake is on the lip of the Salt River Canyon; the highway begins its winding trip to the river below just after it passes the turnoff to Seneca.

*Fishing goes along with camping, and Seneca Lake is a great location for both activities. Ken Akers*

| RECREATION SITE NAME | APPROX. ELEV. | SEASONS OF USE | DAYS-LIMITS | FEE | NO. OF UNITS | SAFE WATER | 16 FT. RV LIMIT | WASTE DISP. | BOATING | FISHING |
|---|---|---|---|---|---|---|---|---|---|---|
| **1** POINT OF PINES LAKE | 6500 | All Yr. | 14 | X | 18 | | X | | X | X |
| **2** SAN CARLOS LAKE | 2800 | All Yr. | none | X | | | | | X | X |
| **3** SENECA LAKE | 4700 | All Yr. | 14 | X | 40 | | | | X | X |

# Southwestern Arizona

Too fat to fly: those top-knotted Gambel's quail at the Organ Pipe Cactus National Monument campground are so big and round they waddle when they walk. The abundant free handouts haven't actually deprived them of the ability to take off, but they look permanently grounded. Sleek coyotes, too, patrol the edges of the big campground, slyly soliciting donations of food, as eager as humans to get something without working for it.

It is winter in the Arizona desert, and visitors from all over the world are camping at Organ Pipe, Painted Rock, and other sun-warmed spots in the southwestern section of the state. They come to escape snow and cold, to immerse themselves in the unique surroundings, to learn about the fragile niches desert flora and fauna have fashioned in the harsh environment. Winter is the most popular season in this land of saguaro and creosote bush, but spring, summer, and fall have their advocates as well, and each offers special reasons to be afield.

Winter means crisp nights and days flooded with sunshine. Warmth to bake out urban ills, to encourage a day-long hike into the foothills, using a desert wash as a highway just like the deer, bobcats, and coyotes whose tracks are there in the sand to guide you. And winter means cheerful, fragrant mesquite fires when the evening chill settles in.

Spring begins the desert year. If winter has left enough moisture, the wildflowers that may have lain dormant for years will burst forth in yellow, red, and blue displays—an unbelievable carnival of color in what appear to be hostile surroundings. In April and May the paloverdes burst into exuberant yellow, and saguaros sprout buds at the tips of their thorny arms. Nights and days are mild; if there's a perfect time to camp, this is it.

Summer brings heat, and most old desert hands have devised ways to avoid it or moderate it. Plants bloom at night and the flowers spread their fragrance beneath the moon. Activity begins at dusk for the desert creatures; beetles, rattlesnakes, kangaroo rats, and foxes come out to dine. Campers who stay quietly in the shade during the day find summer nights are magic. And along the Colorado River you can temper the hot sun by staying wet.

Fall comes slowly and lasts only a short time. Still, late October days are well worth the wait. There is a cool sweetness to the air. The desert harvest is over, but the rising autumn moon is huge and orange, with saguaro silhouetted against its face rather than a shock of corn or a sycamore tree. Camping now is delightful, but largely overlooked except by anglers and hunters who are afield to enjoy nature's fall bounty.

The huge open spaces between Phoenix, Gila Bend, and Yuma are all but empty of people. Rugged desert ranges like the Sand Tank, Sauceda, Eagle Tail, Tinajas Altas, Harcuvar, and Kofa shape the horizons. The land between is mostly dry, with thready ribbons of green along the washes where extra moisture collects. But there is more here than meets the eye. The camper who takes time to get to know the desert, to get closer than a glance out the window of a car speeding down the interstate highway, will find an incredibly rich, busy, and varied world; robust but delicate, old but new, harsh yet friendly. In fact, a camper's world.

*(Above left) Parker Dam on the Colorado backs up the startlingly blue waters of Lake Havasu, a camper's paradise made all the more beautiful by the stark land that surrounds it.* Peter Kresan
*(Right) Brittlebush on the sere landscape of the Cabeza Prieta, along the Mexican border in the southwestern part of Arizona. Thousands of self-contained campers visit favorite desert areas in southwestern Arizona each winter.* Peter Kresan

(Top) Cowboy coffee is an Arizona camping legend.
If it dissolves the spoon, it's just right. James Tallon
(Above) Fat Gambel's quail looking for handouts are
frequent visitors to established desert campgrounds.
They're seldom disappointed. Paul Berquist

(Right) Organ Pipe Cactus National Monument has one
of the largest and most popular desert campgrounds.
Soak up the winter sun and learn about the amazingly
complex Sonoran desert. David Muench

# Early Day Prospecting

About twenty miles up the Gila River from Yuma, the community of Dome basks in the desert sun. It's pretty quiet around here these days—a far cry from that prosperous time in the late 1850s when the boisterous boomtown of Gila City boasted some thousand rough and tumble prospectors. It was Arizona's first gold strike, and the town set the style for other mining camps over the next few years.

Journalist J. Ross Browne, who greatly influenced the style of Mark Twain, wrote of Gila City's heyday in 1859: "Enterprising men hurried to the spot with barrels of whiskey and billiard tables; Jews came with ready-made clothing and fancy wares; traders crowded in with wagonloads of pork and beans; and gamblers came with cards and monte tables. There was everything in Gila City within a few months but a church and a jail...."

Old-timers used to say that when the gold ran out, so did the miners. At last the rich placer diggings began to play out, and the residents of Gila City packed up and moved on. About that time the Gila River went on a rampage, overran its banks, and delivered the coup de grace on what was left of Gila City.

Browne revisited the site during a tour of Arizona in 1863, a year after the flood, and dryly noted the erstwhile boomtown consisted of "three chimneys and a coyote."

But already there had been another big strike not far away. In January, 1862, famed mountain man Pauline Weaver found rich gold placers while trapping on the Colorado River a few miles north of what would become the site of Ehrenberg. Weaver cached a few nuggets in the hollow quill of a goose feather. Shortly afterward, near Yuma, he showed his gold to Jose Redondo, who set out immediately for the new El Dorado. Redondo's first shovelful of dirt panned out a little over two ounces in gold. Thereafter, gold nuggets weighing more than twenty ounces each were apparently fairly common. Another member of the party, Juan Ferrera, was the luckiest of all. In the gulch that bears his name, Ferrera plucked a nugget weighing 47.2 ounces.

The Redondo party named the town that sprung up nearby "La Paz", for it was believed Weaver had made his discovery on January 12, the day honoring our Lady of Peace.

Within a few weeks, hundreds of devil-may-care miners pitched their tents and staked out claims around La Paz. "The population," wrote a California journalist in 1863, "is the worst mixture of Indians, Mexicans, Pikes, and white men from all parts of the earth, I ever saw."

Thieves, when apprehended, were dealt with severely. Isaac Goldberg, a pioneer merchant-freighter, described the punishment given on one instance: "Shortly after my arrival a thief, who had been stealing from stores and other places, was caught. There was, of course, no law officer to confine and try the culprit, so the miners and citizens held a meeting and sentenced him to receive twenty-five lashes. These were promptly and lustily given. After the affair was over, they handed him five dollars in cash, telling him that if he dared to again visit the settlement he would receive a double dose of the same back 'medicine.' You may be sure that the rascal did not return, and that the community was no more troubled by thieves. We could leave all our property unguarded and yet not miss a single cent's worth of anything."

Petty thievery may have been curtailed in La Paz, but a hard look, argument, or the slimmest suspicion of a misdeal was apt to bring the hammer down on forty grains of black powder. Street fights and saloon brawls were as common as cuss words at a muleskinners' convention. It's claimed that the westernmost shooting scrape of the Civil War occurred at La Paz, when a Southern sympathizer shot and killed two Union volunteers.

Those lofty mountains northeast of Yuma, called the Kofas, are the best example of an acronym among Arizona place names. Kofa is derived from the King of Arizona mine, which ran an operation there in the 1890s. The company used a branding iron to stamp its mark on company property. The brand "K of A" became "Kofa," and a new name was born.

## FISH IN A SKILLET

Small trout can be dusted with flour and fried in oil or butter. Try them for a camp breakfast, stuffed with bread crumbs, chopped mushrooms, and bacon bits. Larger trout can be cut along the backbone and butterflied, then grilled over hot coals.

If you're lucky enough to have fresh bass, striper, walleye, or crappie fillets, try them this way:

Pour 1 1/2 to 2 inches of cooking oil into a large, deep skillet. Crush 2 cups corn chips (place in plastic bag and roll with rolling pin), then pour out on a paper towel. In another plastic bag mix 3/4 cup flour, teaspoon seasoned salt, and 1/2 teaspoon lemon pepper. In a bowl beat 3 eggs. Make certain the cooking oil is smoking hot, and try to keep it that way as you cook the fillets. Drop each fillet in the seasoned flour mixture and shake, then dip in the beaten eggs, finally roll in crushed corn chips.

Place the fish in the oil, adding pieces slowly so the oil stays hot. Turn once when golden brown. Do not overcook; the typical fillet takes only a minute or two. The outside should be crisp, the inside moist and flaky.

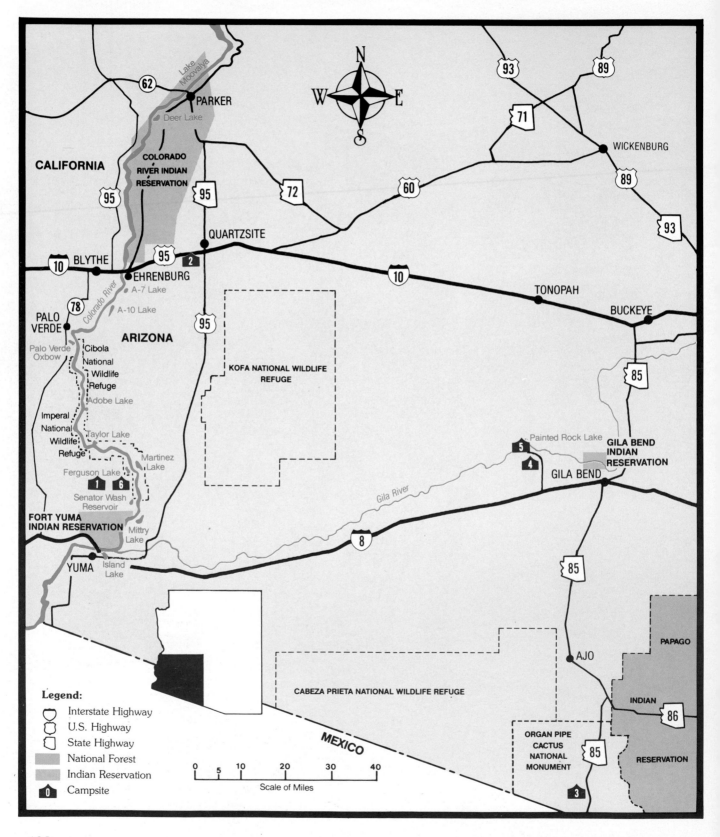

Legend:
- Interstate Highway
- U.S. Highway
- State Highway
- National Forest
- Indian Reservation
- Campsite

# Southwestern Arizona Campsites

Vast areas of this region are reserved for military use as bombing ranges or proving grounds and thus are closed to casual access. A few commercial campgrounds are located along the lower Colorado River, usually in conjunction with marinas or launch areas. So this corner of the state has millions of acres but very few developed campsites.

**Organ Pipe Cactus National Monument** campground is desert camping at its best. The 208 sites are laid out in loops about a mile from monument headquarters, which is on State Route 85 south of Ajo and about 4 miles north of the Mexican border at Lukeville. The campground is open all year. Stay limit is 14 days, January through April; 30 days rest of the year. User fee. Elevation: 1700 feet.

The camp has water; modern restrooms; a dump station for recreational vehicle holding tanks.

**Painted Rock State Historic Park** is one of two state parks in the area. This one began as a day-use area next to a mound of rocks that bears thousands of petroglyphs. It is still best suited to self-contained recreational vehicles. There's room for about 25 vehicles. Fee; 14-day stay limit. No water. Vault-type toilet; a few picnic ramadas with table-bench units. The park is open all year. Elevation is only 735 feet, so summer temperatures usually exceed 110 degrees. Take the Painted Rock exit from Interstate Route 8, about 12 miles west of Gila Bend, then follow the paved access road 15 miles to the park.

**Painted Rock State Recreational Park** is about a mile north of the historic park on the same access road. There is a small lake here — actually the "borrow pit" left from the construction of Painted Rock Dam, a huge earth-fill structure on the Gila River that was built for flood control.

The Arizona State Park campground has 37 sites, with table-bench units and fire pits; about 10 of them have ramadas. Fee; drinking water; modern restrooms and hot showers; 14-day stay limit. Launch ramp; dump station. Open all year. There are a few mesquite and tamarisk trees for shade, but this is real desert camping!

**Squaw Lake** campground is administered by the Bureau of Land Management. It is on the California side of the Colorado River about 23 miles north of Yuma, but is much used by Arizona campers, boaters, and water sports fans. The elevation is only 220 feet, so winter is the most popular season here; but the area is crowded on summer holiday weekends. There are 80 sites, most of them suitable for recreational vehicles. Fee; drinking water; modern restrooms and cold showers; dump station. Boat launch ramp. Table-bench units, some grills; 14-day stay limit. Open all year. A campground host is usually in attendance.

**Imperial Dam**, a collection of 6 separate campgrounds near Squaw Lake on the California side of the Colorado River, is designated by the BLM as a "long-term visitor area" or LTVA. LTVAs are designed for campers with self-contained recreational vehicles. Large, open areas, these sites provide safe water, gray-water disposal, and dump stations, but no shower or toilet facilities. On-site hosts give instructions and assistance. Boating and fishing are within 5 miles; boat ramp is at Senator Wash. Fee; 5-month permit; elevation is 350 feet. Additional open areas for informal camping. From California State 24 turn west onto Senator Wash Road.

In addition to the above campgrounds, there are a number of **informal sites** scattered up and down the Colorado River, often in conjunction with marinas, unimproved access points, or launch ramps.

**La Posa** is an LTVA 1 mile south of Quartzsite, Ariz., on U.S. Route 95. Open year-round, this BLM site is popular with winter visitors. To avoid a crowd, don't arrive during the first week in February when the Quartzsite Pow Wow rock and mineral show draws 30,000 people to the town of 200. La Posa accommodates 4,000 vehicles. Fee; 5-month permit; elevation 850 feet; on-site host. Amenities include dump station, trash pickup, and restrooms.

| RECREATION SITE NAME | APPROX. ELEV. | SEASONS OF USE | DAYS-LIMITS | FEE | NO. OF UNITS | SAFE WATER | 16 FT. RV LIMIT | WASTE DISP. | BOATING | FISHING |
|---|---|---|---|---|---|---|---|---|---|---|
| **1** IMPERIAL DAM | 350 | All Yr. | 150 | X | 1500 | X | | X | X | X |
| **2** LA POSA | 850 | All Yr. | 150 | X | 4000 | X | | X | | |
| **3** ORGAN PIPE CACTUS Nat. Mnmt. | 1700 | All Yr. | 14 | X | 208 | X | | X | | |
| **4** PAINTED ROCK St. Hist. Pk. | 735 | All Yr. | 14 | X | 25 | | | | | |
| **5** PAINTED ROCK St. Rec. Pk. | 735 | All Yr. | 14 | X | 37 | X | | X | X | X |
| **6** SQUAW LAKE | 220 | All Yr. | 14 | X | 80 | X | | X | X | X |

# Southeastern Arizona

Francisco Vasquez de Coronado led his column of explorers to this quiet frontier in 1540, passing through the grassy valleys between soaring ranges, seeking gold he would never find, not recognizing that the land itself was the greatest treasure of all.

The region encompasses a large part of the state and exhibits most of the amazing variety that distinguishes Arizona: the flora, from tiny pincushion cactus to stately pine; the fauna, from desert pupfish to lordly bighorn; successive life zones, from sere desert through oak-grassland to spruce-aspen forest atop 10,700-foot Mount Graham; splendid geography to dazzle the eye and tease the mind, from the jagged outline of the Baboquivari Mountains to nature's whimsical sculpture in the Chiricahuas.

Some parts of this southeastern portion of Arizona resemble other places in the state, but taken as a whole it is unique. The landscape is not flat but rolling: gentle undulations that are bright green when the summer rains begin, a restful buff-tan at other times of the year. It's good cattle and horse country, and the oak draws are hiding places for whitetail deer. There are sycamore and walnut trees, too, and down along the creek near Patagonia you can see how large cottonwoods can grow if left undisturbed.

Then there are the mountain ranges. They seem taller and bulkier than they really are because they thrust upward so abruptly out of the countryside. You do not approach an ascent gradually; the road is on the plain one minute, zigzagging up the flank of the mountain the next.

There are campgrounds in these broad-shouldered mountains; shady glens tucked back in canyon recesses or perched on unexpected mesas. Campsites on the southern slopes of the Santa Catalinas look down on Tucson and its valley full of people. But from the top of the Chiricahuas or regal Mount Graham, you can look out 200 miles and — except for a few scattered lights at night — discern no sign of man's hand.

As in most parts of Arizona, campers here have a choice: you can seek out the tables and grills, water and restrooms of improved campgrounds or simply find your own camp spot. It might be in the luxuriant desert between Florence and Tucson, with its parkway specially signed to identify cactus, trees, and shrubs. (Choose a weekend when the moon is full and enjoy a nightly coyote concerto. A chorus of a dozen members, each trying to outdo the other, is guaranteed to add an eerie quality to your evening campfire.) Or you might wander off to one of the remote ranges such as the Peloncillos, Galiuros, or Dragoons, assured that your nearest neighbor will be miles away.

It's easy to move up and down the life-zone scale in this region. If it's January and the upper levels of the mountain ranges are covered with snow, set up camp at Patagonia Lake, in the sunshine of Gilbert Ray, or along the lakeshore at Roper. In May consider the pleasant confines of Rucker Canyon or the oaks at Peña Blanca. In the heat of summer you can flee to the cool shade at Spencer Canyon, Riggs Flat, or Rustler Park.

Coronado was the original explorer, but many other pioneers have followed in the four centuries since to add to the special flavor of this region. When you camp anywhere in Coronado country, you can feel the spirit of the miners of Tombstone and Harshaw and Ruby; the troopers who pursued Cochise and Geronimo through the rugged defiles of the Chiricahuas; the ranchers like Henry Hooker and Ed Riggs and Pete Kitchen who were the first permanent settlers. Their ghosts still ride the ridgeline.

*(Above left) Accomplished burro beggars at Picacho Peak State Park. James Tallon*
*(Right) Patagonia Lake is tucked into a fold of this rolling, high desert landscape northeast of Nogales. Elevation here is 4000 feet, so temperatures are pleasant year-round. Willard Clay*

(Above) Nature's balancing act on display at Chiricahua National Monument. Peter Kresan

(Left) Small streams create mini-Niagaras in many ranges in the southeastern corner of the state. Ed Cooper

(Right) The pleasant campground at Chiricahua National Monument is tucked away in a grove of trees not far from monument headquarters. Art Clark

(Below) Wind, water, and time combined to produce these dramatic sculptures in the Chiricahuas. Peter Kresan

(Above) Hurry, Daddy, I know the fish are waiting.
Jeff Kida
(Left) Mount Graham is a huge, forested island in the
desert country south and west of Safford. Its high, cool
pine forest has been popular with summer campers since
the first settlers came to the Gila River Valley a century
ago. David Muench
(Below) Riggs Flat Lake, atop Mount Graham, has
a Coronado National Forest campground nearby.
Dick Dietrich

# Campfire Recipes

### TEA AND SYMPATHY

Day hike lunch: remove the lid from a Number 10 can and clean it. Inside, pack a styrofoam cup for each person, tea bags or envelopes of instant soup. Elsewhere in your day pack or fanny pack: a small jar of peanut butter and an apple for each person; or crackers and cheese, or crackers and a can of corned beef. When it's lunch time, start a very small fire with twigs and heat water in the can. Slice apples and cover each slice with peanut butter or fix crackers with cheese or beef. Wash down with hot tea or soup.

# The Outlaw King of Old Galeyville

*Around the Campfire*

The genesis of Galeyville, on the eastern side of the Chiricahua Mountains, was similar to that of many another short-lived boomtown in Cochise County.

In this case it all started in 1880 when John Galey arrived from Pennsylvania to promote a silver mine. Since the prospect was only sixty miles, as the crow flies, from Tombstone's bonanza, Galey visualized himself as the next silver king of Arizona. He secured some financial backing and laid out a townsite. Before long, Galeyville boasted eleven saloons and some thirty other various and sundry enterprises.

The boom lasted only about a year. The silver played out, and Galeyville became another metropolis that didn't quite "metrop." The story of old Galeyville might have ended right there, had not a pack of outlaws led by Curly Bill Brocius decided to take up residence.

Curly Bill, whose real name was William Brocius Graham, was the bandit chieftain in these parts. He wore a white hat that contrasted sharply with his dark curly hair, black eyes, and swarthy complexion. The boisterous, devil-may-care reprobate was considered a popular, swashbuckling figure by friend and foe alike, and nobody disputed his reputation as outlaw king of Galeyville, or the whole of Cochise County for that matter.

Curly Bill, who was given his nickname by a dark-eyed senorita from Mexico, didn't discriminate. He robbed Mexicans and Anglos with equal enthusiasm. It's been said the gregarious outlaw was a kind of frontier Robin Hood, who stole only from the rich. If Curly Bill stole only from the rich, it was because there was no profit in stealing from the poor. His targets included trains, stagecoaches, and borderland smugglers. His favorite enterprise, however, was cattle rustling. In those days, the U.S. Army was paying hard cash for beef on the hoof, and nobody bothered to inspect the brands.

Curly Bill had a loose-knit partnership with Cochise County's unscrupulous sheriff, Johnny Behan. Behan conveniently looked the other way when Brocius pulled his capers, and when the sheriff's tax collector, Bill Breakenridge, came to Galeyville, the outlaw helped take up the collection from local residents.

This unholy alliance almost got Curly Bill planted in six feet of Galeyville sod. When a tough outlaw from the Pecos River country named Jim Wallace rode into town looking for a job, Curly Bill brought him into the gang. Wallace claimed that he rode with Billy the Kid in the Lincoln County War and had no love for lawmen. He declared they were as welcome in his camp as a sheepman at a cattlemen's convention. When Billy Breakenridge arrived to collect taxes, Wallace took one jaundiced look at the deputy's badge, made some threatening remarks, then drew his six-gun.

Curly Bill stepped in and ordered Wallace to holster his shooting iron and apologize.

"No Lincoln County hoss thief can come in here and abuse Billy," he warned. "Breakenridge is our deputy, and that suits us."

For a spell it looked like the matter was settled. The three went into the nearest saloon and shared a bottle of whiskey.

After a few drinks, however, Curly Bill turned surly. Suddenly he jerked out his six-shooter and threatened to plug Wallace. Bloodshed was avoided when several of the boys separated the pair.

Wallace stomped out of the saloon, went to the stable, and got his horse. He rode back up the street, dismounted, and waited outside the saloon for Curly Bill. When Brocius stepped out through the swinging doors and saw what was happening, he went for his gun. Wallace had already drawn his, and had it resting on his horse's neck. A shot rang out, and Curly Bill went down with a bullet hole through his cheek.

Several members of Bill's gang grabbed Wallace and started to string him up; but when it looked like Curly Bill would survive, they let him go. Bill lost a couple of teeth, and had to spend the next few weeks with an awkward bandage tied around his head to keep his jaw in place. Otherwise he was no worse for wear.

Curly Bill figured prominently in many nefarious doings along the Mexican border in the early 1880s. He was personally responsible for rustling thousands of Mexican longhorns, and earned the dubious distinction of having his name mentioned in a number of warmly worded diplomatic notes exchanged between the United States and Mexico.

The outlaw's undoing came in the spring of 1882 when he mixed it up with the Earp brothers and Doc Holliday at Mescal Springs. Wyatt Earp claimed that, during an exchange of shots, he downed the outlaw chief with a blast from his twin-barreled scattergun. Curly Bill's cronies always insisted their leader was never at Mescal Springs, but in Mexico with his sweetheart at the time.

There was so much controversy over the matter that a Tombstone newspaper, friendly to Curly Bill's wild bunch, offered a thousand-dollar reward to anyone who could produce the corpse of Curly Bill. The other Tombstone paper, siding with Wyatt, countered by offering a thousand dollars for the live body of Curly Bill. Neither side ever collected.

---

## SOUNDS TERRIBLE, TASTES GREAT

If your camp meal includes dark meat such as venison, duck, or dove — or even if you have to settle for beef — here's a simple and tasty sauce: mix equal parts of burgundy wine, catsup, and red currant jelly. Stir in saucepan and heat over low flame. Have faith: the result is terrific.

## LAST BUT NOT LEAST

The foil trick also works well with hamburgers, many campers' favorite meal. Add thin slices of raw potatoes, carrots, and onions to the package, and season with salt and pepper. You have a complete meal, all cooked at the same time — with no dishes to wash.

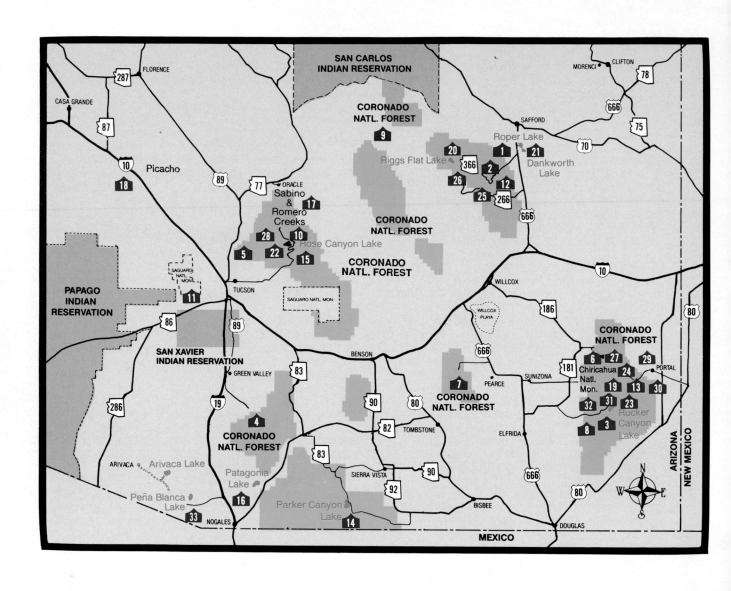

NOTE: Fees, seasons of use, weather, etc.,
can cause changes in the availability of
camping facilities. For updated information
on this region, see agency addresses and
phone numbers listed inside the back cover.

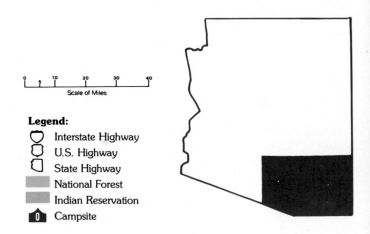

Scale of Miles

**Legend:**
- Interstate Highway
- U.S. Highway
- State Highway
- National Forest
- Indian Reservation
- Campsite

# Southeastern Arizona Campsites

**White Rock** is the U. S. Forest Service campground at Peña Blanca Lake. From Interstate Route 19, about 6 miles north of Nogales, turn west and travel 10 paved miles through stands of oaks and rolling grassland. Elevation here is 4000 feet. The 15 sites have table-bench units, and most are shaded by large oaks. Fee; water; restrooms; 14-day stay limit. Open all year. You'll find a store, cafe, motel, and rental boats at the lake.

**Patagonia Lake** campground is part of the Arizona State Parks system. It offers 10 sites with water and electric hookups; 24 sites with table-bench-grill units; and 136 undeveloped camping spots. Fee; drinking water; 14-day stay limit. Modern restrooms with hot showers and a dump station.

There also are 14 sites located along the shore, accessible only by boat. Elevation here is 4000 feet. Access is via State Route 82 from Patagonia or Nogales. The park is open all year. Store, rental boats, launch ramp, swimming beach.

**Lakeview** campground sits on a ridge overlooking Parker Canyon Lake. This is part of the Coronado National Forest, with an elevation of 5400 feet; the landscape is dotted with oak and juniper. There are 64 sites in two loops. Fee; water; table-bench units; restrooms. Open all year. Trailers longer than 32 feet prohibited. Access is via State Route 83 southwest of Sonoita, the last 20 miles unpaved. Also at the lake are a store, rental boats, and a free launch ramp.

**Cochise Stronghold** is in the Dragoon Moun-

| RECREATION SITE NAME | APPROX. ELEV. | SEASONS OF USE | DAYS-LIMITS | FEE | NO. OF UNITS | SAFE WATER | 16 FT. RV LIMIT | WASTE DISP. | BOATING | FISHING |
|---|---|---|---|---|---|---|---|---|---|---|
| 1 ARCADIA | 6700 | May Nov. | 14 | X | 18 | X | X | | | |
| 2 UPPER ARCADIA | 6700 | May Nov. | 14 | X | 2 | X | X | | | |
| 3 BATHTUB | 6300 | All Yr. | 14 | X | 11 | X | X | | | X |
| 4 BOG SPRINGS | 5600 | All Yr. | 14 | X | 13 | X | | | | |
| 5 CATALINA ST. PARK | 2650 | All Yr. | 14 | X | 50 | X | | X | | |
| 6 CHIRICAHUA Nat. Monument | 5400 | All Yr. | 14 | X | 26 | X | | | | |
| 7 COCHISE STRONGHOLD | 5000 | All Yr. | 14 | X | 23 | X | X | | | |
| 8 CYPRESS PARK | 6000 | Mar. Oct. | 14 | X | 7 | X | X | X | | X |
| 9 FOUR-MILE CAMPGROUND | 2900 | All Yr. | 14 | | 10 | X | | | | |
| 10 GENERAL HITCHCOCK | 6000 | Apr. Oct. | 14 | | 13 | X | X | | | |
| 11 GILBERT RAY | 2600 | All Yr. | 7 | X | 160 | X | | | | |
| 12 HOSPITAL FLAT | 9000 | May Nov. | 14 | X | 12 | X | | | | |
| 13 IDLEWILD | 5000 | Apr. Oct. | 14 | X | 10 | X | | | | |
| 14 LAKEVIEW | 5400 | All Yr. | 14 | X | 64 | X | | | X | X |
| 15 MOLINO BASIN | 4500 | Oct. Apr. | 14 | | 49 | | | | | |
| 16 PATAGONIA LAKE | 4000 | All Yr. | 14 | X | 184 | X | | X | X | X |
| 17 PEPPERSAUCE | 4700 | All Yr. | 14 | | 31 | X | | | | |
| 18 PICACHO PEAK | 2000 | All Yr. | 14 | X | 31 | X | | | | |

| RECREATION SITE NAME | APPROX. ELEV. | SEASONS OF USE | DAYS-LIMITS | FEE | NO. OF UNITS | SAFE WATER | 16 FT. RV LIMIT | WASTE DISP. | BOATING | FISHING |
|---|---|---|---|---|---|---|---|---|---|---|
| 19 PINERY CANYON | 7000 | Apr. Nov. | 14 | | 5 | | X | | | |
| 20 RIGGS FLAT | 8600 | May Nov. | 14 | X | 26 | X | X | | X | X |
| 21 ROPER LAKE | 3100 | All Yr. | 14 | X | 22 | X | | X | X | X |
| 22 ROSE CANYON* | 7000 | Apr. Oct. | 14 | X | 98 | X | | | | X |
| 23 RUCKER LAKE | 6300 | All Yr. | 14 | X | 9 | X | | | X | X |
| 23A Camp Rucker* | 5600 | All Yr. | 14 | X | 9 | X | X | X | | |
| 23B Rucker Forest Camp | 6500 | All Yr. | 14 | X | 14 | X | | | | |
| 24 RUSTLER PARK | 8500 | Apr. Nov. | 14 | X | 25 | X | X | | | |
| 25 SHANNON | 9100 | May Nov. | 14 | X | 10 | X | X | | | |
| 26 SOLDIER CREEK | 9300 | May Nov. | 14 | X | 11 | X | | | | |
| 27 SOUTH FORK | 5300 | All Yr. | 14 | | 4 | X | | | | |
| 28 SPENCER CANYON* | 8000 | Apr. Oct. | 14 | X | 60 | X | | | | |
| 29 STEWART | 5000 | All Yr. | 14 | X | 6 | X | | | | |
| 30 SUNNY FLAT | 5200 | All Yr. | 14 | X | 11 | X | | | | |
| 31 SYCAMORE | 6200 | All Yr. | 14 | | 5 | X | | | | |
| 32 WEST TURKEY CREEK | 5900 | All Yr. | 14 | | 7 | | | | | |
| 33 WHITE ROCK* | 4000 | All Yr. | 14 | X | 15 | X | | | X | X |

* Sites with handicapped facilities.

# Campsites

tains, 7 miles west of the tiny community of Pearce. The campground has 23 sites. Fee; water; table-bench units; restrooms; 14-day stay limit. Open all year. Trailers restricted to those less than 16 feet long. Firewood is scarce, so bring your own.

**Cypress Park** is one of three small Forest Service campgrounds in Rucker Canyon on the western side of the Chiricahua range. It's about 23 miles east of Elfrida via a county road. Cypress has 7 sites. User fee; drinking water; restrooms. Open March through October; 14-day stay limit. Trailers larger than 16 feet are not allowed. Sites are shaded by large oak trees, and there are some Arizona cypress trees along the nearby creek. Elevation is 6000 feet.

**Bathtub** campground is just up the road from Cypress and just below Rucker Lake. The thick stand of trees and lack of maneuvering room make recreational vehicle access impossible, so Bathtub is for tents and small pickup campers. Fee; water; restrooms. Open year-round; 14-day stay limit.

Three campgrounds are within range of good spring and summer trout fishing at Rucker Lake, a small lake that sparkles in the cool, green canyon. All are open year-round and restricted to recreational vehicles 16 feet and less. **Camp Rucker** has 9 sites. Fee; water; a 14-day stay limit; facilities for the handicapped. The campground named **Rucker Lake** also has 9 units. Fee; water (turned off in winter); 14-day stay limit; restrooms. At an elevation of 6500 feet, **Rucker Forest Camp** has 14 units. Fee; water (turned off in winter); restrooms; table-bench units; 14-day stay limit.

**West Turkey Creek** is in a shady canyon on the western side of the Chiricahua Mountains, north of Rucker and approximately 23 miles northeast of Elfrida, with access by unpaved road. Seven sites; table-bench units; restrooms. No drinking water; no fee. Trailers limited to 16 feet. Open all year with a 14-day stay limit. Elevation is 5900 feet.

**Sycamore** campground is also on Turkey Creek, a mile farther east. Five sites, restrooms, but no drinking water. No fee. Season is all year; elevation is 6200 feet. Trailers limited to 16 feet. Turkey Creek flows most of the year, and there is luxuriant growth in the canyon, including many species of trees.

**Chiricahua National Monument** celebrates the fantastic rock formations in the northern end of this mountain range. The National Park Service has provided a 26-site campground just up the road from the visitor center. Fee; table-bench units; modern restrooms. Ten of the sites can handle trailers up to 22 feet in length. Campground is open all year; stay limit is 14 days. The park is southeast of Willcox via State Route 186.

**Idlewild** is one of four small campgrounds along Cave Creek on the eastern side of the Chiricahuas, 2 miles west of Portal. Ten sites; water; restrooms. User fee. Trailers up to 22 feet permitted. Campground open April through October. Elevation: 5000 feet.

**Stewart** is another of the Cave Creek campgrounds, 2 miles from Portal. Six sites; water; restrooms. User fee. Open year-round, with a 14-day stay limit. Trailers limited to 16 feet. Elevation: 5000 feet.

**Sunny Flat**, a mile farther up Cave Creek, has 11 sites. Fee; water; restrooms. Open year-round. Trailers to 22 feet permitted. Elevation: 5200 feet.

**South Fork** campground is 4 miles from Portal. Four sites; table-bench units; restroom. No drinking water; no fee; recreational vehicles not allowed. Open year-round; stay limit, 14 days.

**Pinery Canyon** is 9 miles southeast of Chiricahua National Monument. Five sites; restrooms. No drinking water; no fee. Season is April through November, with the usual 14-day stay limit. No trailers over 16 feet are permitted. Elevation: 7000 feet.

**Rustler Park**, also on the eastern side of the Chiricahuas, is at 8500 feet, about 8 miles from Portal. User fee; 25 cool sites; drinking water. Season is April through November, with a stay limit of 14 days. Trailers permitted up to 16 feet.

**Shannon** campground is situated on the Swift Trail from Safford to the top of Mount Graham. You ascend from 3000 feet to more than 9000 feet, with matchless views along the way. Shannon has 10 sites, water, and allows trailers to 16 feet. User fee. The season is May through November. Elevation: 9100 feet.

**Hospital Flat**, at 9000 feet, offers 12 sites with drinking water, fee. No trailers allowed; for tent campers only. Season is May-November, with a stay limit of 14 days.

**Soldier Creek** is the next camp up the road, 37 miles from Safford. User fee; 11 sites; water and restrooms. Trailers permitted up to 22 feet. Season is May-November, with a 14-day stay limit. Elevation is 9300 feet, so look for frost even in August.

**Four-Mile** campground, 15 miles west of Safford on U.S. Route 70 then 30 miles southwest to Klon-

*Catalina State Park, on the northwest slope of the Catalina Mountains near Tucson, has some excellent hiking trails.* Peter Kresan

# Campsites

dike, is popular as an overnight stop for people heading in and out of Aravaipa Canyon. The 10-unit campground has safe water, flush toilets and cold showers, and table-bench units. No fee; 14-day stay limit; open all year. The elevation is 2900 feet. Campers are encouraged to provide their own shade.

**Riggs Flat** is the most popular Mount Graham campground because of the pretty little trout lake nearby. This is close to the end of the road, at 8600 feet; you're about 41 miles from Safford. The campground has 26 sites. Fee; water; table-bench units; restrooms. Trailers up to 22 feet are allowed. Season is normally May-November, with a 14-day stay limit. The pattern of winter snows may add or subtract a few weeks at either end of this period. Trout fishing requires a trout stamp.

**Arcadia**, 19 miles southwest of Safford off U.S. Route 666 and State Route 366, has 18 units and restricts trailers to 16 feet. **Upper Arcadia**, around the corner, is a 2-unit site with a group area. Trailers are not allowed. For both Arcadias there is a fee and a 14-day stay limit. Both have restrooms, water, and table-bench-grill units. Season is May 15-November 15.

**Roper Lake** is part of the Arizona State Parks system, and the campground is right on the shore. There are actually 3 camping areas, including a group area, with a total of 100 campsites. Thirty-two sites have water and electricity hookups, and some are pull-through. Drinking water; modern restrooms; hot showers; ramadas; special programs, picnic sites. User fee; 14-day stay limit. At this elevation (3100 feet) summer temperatures can reach 100 degrees. Open all year, you'll need an electricity hookup to keep warm in the winter. Turnoff to the park (paved access) is from U.S. Route 666 just south of Safford.

**Peppersauce** campground is on the back side of the Santa Catalina range, south of Oracle about 15 miles via unpaved Forest Road 382. There are 31 sites here at an elevation of 4700 feet. No fee; water; 14-day stay limit. Open all year.

**Molino Basin** is the first of several campgrounds along the paved highway leading from Tucson to the top of Mount Lemmon in the Catalinas. Eighteen miles from the city, it has 49 sites with table-bench units, restrooms, but no drinking water. No fee; 14-day stay limit. Trailers longer than 22 feet are not permitted.

**General Hitchcock** is the next campground up the mountain, 21 miles from Tucson. There are 13 sites here, with table-bench units and restrooms. There is water, but no fee. The season is April through October, with a 14-day stay limit. Elevation is 6000 feet. Trailers are not permitted.

**Rose Canyon**, largest campground on Mount Lemmon, has 98 sites. Fee; drinking water; table-bench units; restrooms. The season is April through October, with a 14-day stay limit. Besides the chance to cool off and relax, the big attraction here is the small lake nearby stocked with rainbow trout from April-October. Rose Canyon is 33 miles from Tucson, at an elevation of 7000 feet.

**Spencer Canyon** campground, 39 miles from Tucson, is almost at the top of Mount Lemmon at 8000 feet. There are 60 campsites here, with table-bench units, drinking water, and restrooms. User fee. The campground is open from April to October, with a 14-day stay limit. Trailers up to 22 feet are permitted.

**Gilbert Ray** campground is part of the Pima County Parks system. It's located in the Tucson Mountains about 8 miles west of the city and is reached via Ajo Way or Speedway Boulevard. Two loops totaling 134 sites offer electric hookups, a water supply, and modern restrooms. Twenty-six other sites have table-bench units suitable for tent camping or self-contained recreational vehicles. Fee; year-round season; 7-day stay limit. Elevation: 2600 feet. The western unit of Saguaro National Monument is nearby; so are the Arizona-Sonora Desert Museum and Old Tucson.

**Bog Springs** is on the western slope of the Santa Rita Mountains in Madera Canyon. The campground is 13 miles east of Green Valley and Interstate Route 19, and access is paved. There are 13 sites, with table-bench units, drinking water, and restrooms. User fee; 14-day stay limit. Trailers longer than 22 feet are not allowed. Elevation: 5600 feet. Open all year.

**Picacho Peak** is another unit of the Arizona State Parks system. The famed landmark is beside Interstate Route 10 about 35 miles north of Tucson. There are 31 campsites here, 19 with electric and water hookups. Another 7 sites have table-bench-grill units. Modern restrooms; hot showers; 14-day stay limit. The park also offers picnic sites where no camping is allowed. Park roads are paved, and recreational vehicles of all sizes can be accommodated. Fee varies according to facilities used. Elevation: 2000 feet. A hiking trail leads to the summit of Picacho Peak.

**Catalina State Park** snuggles up to the western base of the Santa Catalina Mountain range in some of the most spectacular desert scenery anywhere. The elevation is 2650 feet, so fall, winter, and spring temperatures are perfect. Even during the warmer summer months the nights are pleasant. There are 50 undeveloped camping sites, a central water supply, modern restroom, and a dump station. The park is open all year with a 14-day stay limit. The usual state park fees apply. There's a special equestrian area, and both horsemen and hikers enjoy the miles of trails within the park and on the adjoining Coronado National Forest land. Access is from U.S. Route 89 just a few miles north of the Tucson city limits.

*James Tallon*

# Camping Tips

Here's a collection of ideas and suggestions you may find useful on your next camping trip.

• Forget the grill? Bend a wire coat hanger into a rectangular shape, cover with foil—and start cookin'!

• Most soap won't remove fishy odors from hands, and the smell of salmon eggs is nearly impossible to remove. Try tomato juice, rubbing alcohol, lemon juice, or baking soda—or rub some toothpaste on your hands. Yes, toothpaste!

• Aluminum pie pans make good camp plates. They're stronger than paper plates, can be reused, and withstand the rough and tumble of packing and unpacking.

• If you're going to cook over an open fire, coat the bottom of pots and pans with liquid soap. Afterwards the black from the fire will wash right off—no scrubbing needed.

• The kind of wood you use for a cooking fire is important. In Arizona, oak, mesquite, walnut, and juniper are best. Pine is smoky and sooty, and it doesn't leave long-lasting coals, so it should be your last choice. Good firewood is hard to find around many campgrounds, and in some areas permits are required. Consider bringing a supply from home for a special cooking fire.

• Bake potatoes ahead of time. If you cook them at home and freeze them, they need only be heated at camp. Or cook them three-quarters done and wrap in foil; then finish them on the grill or in the campfire coals. About twenty minutes will have them ready for the table.

• A wire or plastic milk case can stow camp gear, be a grub box, serve as a seat in camp, or stand in as a mini-table for ice chest or water cooler. The cases stack easily for storage and loading, too.

• Never drive nails into standing timber. To hang pots, pans, jackets, a mirror, and so forth, tie a piece of rope around the tree and attach snap-open rings, the kind used for shower curtains.

• "Pack it in, pack it out" should be a golden rule for campers. Take along some large plastic garbage bags. Clean up the area when you arrive and again just before you leave. Smokey the Bear and your fellow campers will bless you.

• If you're taking charcoal, fill an empty half-gallon milk carton with briquets; staple it shut for neat and easy transport. When you're ready to cook, light the entire carton.

• Additional uses for garbage bags: cut one open and use as a ground cloth under a tent or sleeping bag. Cut arm and head holes to make an emergency raincoat. Open and use as a tablecloth (secure it with masking tape). Using some care and ingenuity, fashion a tent from three or four of the bags.

• A nylon hammock is handy if you dislike sleeping on the ground. It especially appeals to backpackers, since it weighs almost nothing and can be rolled up in a fist-sized ball.

• If you hate to get up to fix breakfast on a chilly morning, prepare a thermos the night before with instant oatmeal, hot water, powdered cream, and sugar. Placed within easy reach, it will help your heart get started. Fill a second thermos with hot coffee and you can sleep an extra half-hour.

• If you forget to take soap on a camping trip, you can make an acceptable substitute from bacon grease and wood ashes. You'll be clean, but you may smell like breakfast all day long.

• One of those compressed fireplace logs can provide a dozen or more campfire starters. Slice off a one-inch chunk, build a small teepee of kindling, and light the piece of log beneath it.

• Wear glasses? To find them quickly in the dark, fasten some Velcro to the tent seam or recreational vehicle wall just above your bed, another piece to your glasses case.

• Use a mesh bag to dip dishes into very hot rinse water; to hang food in trees out of reach of animals; as a kit for toiletries; or, filled with rocks, as an emergency boat anchor.

• To start a campfire quickly, pour leftover cooking grease on the kindling. Smells good, too.

• Breakfast treat: for each person, cut an orange in two and scoop out the pulp. Break an egg into each half of the empty orange shell, wrap in foil, and cook in hot coals for five minutes. Meanwhile, put the orange pulp in a plastic bag and squeeze out the juice.

• A loose wad of steel wool makes a good emergency fire starter. It flames with one match and burns hot.

• If you intend to cook over an open fire, pound three iron rods into the ground to form a triangle before you start the fire. You can set your skillet or pot on the rod ends and not worry about a grill.

• If you're having French toast for breakfast, let the bread dry out overnight.

• Don't wear your "day clothes" to bed. For comfortable sleeping, flannel pajamas are much better (or even no clothes at all.)

# Camping Tips

- More garbage-bag ideas: put one heavy-duty bag inside another, half fill with water, and hang from a tree limb. When the sun has warmed the water, poke a dozen holes in the bottom of the bag and take a shower in the woods.
- Apply insect repellent the easy way: pop the ball off an empty roll-on deodorant bottle, rinse well, and refill with liquid repellent.
- Backpackers can make a light, handy wash basin from a gallon plastic jug. Cut off three or four inches from the bottom.
- New flavor for fried fish: dip fillets in beaten egg-milk mixture, roll in flour, again in the egg, then in pretzel crumbs. Fry in hot oil.
- Crumpled aluminum foil works well for scrubbing pots. It cleans up grills nicely, too.
- If you're stung by a mosquito or bee, sprinkle some meat tenderizer on the bite; the pain will ease immediately.
- Remove the labels from empty pill bottles and use them to store small, easily damaged articles such as matches, safety pins, lantern mantles, toothpicks, and so forth.
- To make your ice chest more efficient, fashion a slip cover from foam carpet padding. Cut to fit loosely; glue pieces together.
- Repair the torn netting in tent windows with bridal veil material, available at most fabric stores.
- A good, moisture-proof container for a roll of toilet paper is an empty one-pound coffee can complete with snap-on lid.
- Freeze water in two-liter soft drink bottles, half-gallon milk cartons, or gallon plastic jugs to keep the ice chest cold but dry. When the ice melts you still have a backup water supply.
- While it's daylight, check the zippers of your sleeping bags and lubricate with light oil, WD-40, or candle wax.
- An old aluminum ski pole makes a dandy hiking or wading staff—a good "third leg."
- Rinse a quart milk carton and use it to store eggs for camp use. Break them into the carton; they will pour out one at a time.
- If your feet are always cold at night, try putting the bottom third of your sleeping bag into a big garbage bag. Don't tie or tape the garbage bag; leave it loose so moisture can escape.
- More on cold feet: wool socks help, of course; so does a hot water bottle. A rock, heated and wrapped in a towel, or a canteen filled with hot water makes an effective emergency warmer.
- Modern sleeping bags filled with man-made fibers such as Hollofill or Dacron-88 can be washed on the gentle cycle, then tumbled dry without hurting their insulating properties. Consider making a sleeping-bag liner from an old sheet—it's much easier to wash than the entire bag.
- Highway flares make good fire starters, especially when wood is damp. The short, fifteen-minute flares are inexpensive.
- To warm up in cold weather, drink hot liquids such as soup, coffee, tea, or cocoa. Alcoholic drinks lower the body temperature and make you colder.
- Disposable butane lighters are more dependable than matches. Keep several around camp; carry in backpacks and in vehicle glove compartments.
- An excellent camp toaster: Drill a number of holes in the bottom of an 8-by-8-inch cake pan and set a square of 1/4-inch wire mesh on top. The campfire, propane stove, or gas burner will give you nicely browned toast.
- Keep canteens and thermos bottles clean and sweet with a tablespoon or two of baking soda dissolved in water. Let stand, then rinse.
- Disposable washcloths from the supermarket's baby-product section are perfect for quick cleanups in camp. Good for removing fish smells from hands, too.
- Keep several cans of tomato juice on hand in camp, in case your dog has a run-in with a skunk. Bathing the pet in the juice should remove most of the odor.
- To make a gas lantern directional, line half or more of the inside of the globe with aluminum foil. This will reflect and channel the light in a specific direction.
- To keep fish from sticking to the skillet, add a bit of vinegar to the cooking oil.
- If the leather washer in your camp stove has dried out (of course you discover this in camp—a long way from home), you can lubricate it with oil from the car engine dip stick, with butter or cooking oil, or even with a bit of bacon grease.
- To make a camp stove, cut a 30-gallon oil drum in half horizontally. In the bottom half drill several two-inch holes about six inches above the base. With a good blaze going, this demidrum will put out much more heat than a campfire; if you add a grill on top, it becomes a cook stove as well.
- To get rid of those tiny, nearly invisible cactus spines, try spreading hair remover over them. Wait

# Camping Tips

ten minutes and wipe off; the spines should be gone. Hospital emergency rooms often use this method.

• To make a compact stove for cooking or heat, fill a one- or two-pound coffee can with tightly coiled corrugated cardboard. Melt paraffin (highly flammable; do not melt over open flame) and pour into the can, soaking the cardboard. Store with lid on tight. To use, simply light with a match for a hot, long-burning source of heat.

• Old newspapers have many campsite uses. Place them beneath your sleeping bag for extra insulation. Put a stack at the entrance to your tent or recreational vehicle and peel off a few layers to keep the "door mat" clean, to wrap blackened pots for the trip home to the dishwasher, as padding for loose objects when you pack your gear. Tape some together for a tablecloth (you can read while you eat). And of course they can even be used to help start fires.

• To keep the thermos bottles from rolling around on the floorboard of your vehicle (and perhaps shattering), try a fire-extinguisher holder. Install it on the firewall under the dashboard and clamp the thermos securely. If the fit isn't quite right, add a piece of foam rubber to make it snug.

• A cold head means a cold body. Wear a stocking cap to bed on chilly nights and you'll sleep better.

• Most campers wash dishes as one of the last chores before breaking camp. Use the dishwater to douse the fire—one more time—then stir and douse again. Be sure the ashes are stone-cold before you leave.

• Camp flashlights do a lot of loafing between trips. To be sure the batteries are always ready, reverse one of them in the case until you're ready to use the flashlight. And store an extra light bulb by wrapping it in tissue and inserting it in the spring at the bottom of the flashlight.

• If you have a tarp with no grommets or other places to tie a rope, fold a small, smooth rock in the canvas and twist, then tie just beyond the stone. Don't use a rock with sharp edges.

• To protect saw blades and the cutting edges of hatchets or axes, split lengths of old garden hose and slip over the blades. This will keep tools sharp and help prevent accidents.

• Here's an easy way to tell how much time remains until sundown. Hold your hand flat with fingers extended and line it up between the bottom of the sun and the horizon. Each finger width represents fifteen minutes.

• If you're worried about youngsters getting lost in the woods around camp, equip each one with a referee's whistle—with strict instructions not to blow it unless he or she is in trouble. The sound carries much better than shouting.

• A box of baking soda kept in the refrigerator of your recreational vehicle will absorb odors. Put a teaspoon of soda in the fresh-water holding tank of your vehicle, or mix a box with water and flush into the toilet holding tank. For cool, dry feet, sprinkle some soda in your hiking boots.

• Waterproof matches by dipping them in thin shellac. It makes them burn better, too. Store the treated matches in 35mm film containers

• Use strong plastic bags as mixing bowls: put flour, milk, and other ingredients in a plastic bag, mix well by squeezing the bag, then cut off one corner to make a pouring spout.

• Melt old candles and pour the paraffin into paper cups or fiber egg-carton sections half filled with sawdust; mix, adding pieces of heavy cotton cord for wicks. These make excellent fire starters.

• Dip large pine cones in melted paraffin or old candle wax to make good fire starters that also crackle cheerfully and burn with brilliant colors.

• The thick layer of decaying needles and leaves on the forest floor, called "duff," may be several inches thick. It must be cleared down to bare dirt to ensure a safe campfire; otherwise a spark might smolder for days, then burst into flame when nudged by the wind.

• Be sure your camp gear includes some guidebooks on the plants, rocks, birds, and other animals of the region. Take time to get acquainted with your outdoor neighbors and their native environment.

J. Peter Mortimer

126

# Index

Pages that are **boldface** denote pictures
Page followed by an "m" denotes map
*Italics* denote recipes

# Index

*Sunset at Patagonia Lake State Park, a very popular winter campground.* J. Peter Mortimer